The Pyramid Approach to Education: Lesson Plans for Young Children Volume One

Edited by
Andy Bondy, Ph.D.

with contributions by
Kate Dickey
Sarah Buswell
Beth Sulzer-Azaroff, Ph.D.

Table of Contents

Acknowledgements

I would like to thank Andy Bondy for his continued support, guidance, and his everlasting patience. I would like to thank Lori Frost for her communicative expertise and creativity. A very special thank you goes to Sarah Buswell for her tireless hours of constructing functional lesson plans in which to successfully instruct children. Additionally, thank you to Mindy Glassberg for her invaluable pre-school teaching experience and insights. Thank you to Scott Helsinger and the ReMed staff for their contribution of ideas regarding a seemingly endless matrix of skills and activities. But mostly, I want to thank my family for their enduring love and encouragement and through which all things are possible.
Kate Dickey

Preface

The purpose of this manual is to provide a resource for parents, teachers, aides, and other individuals working with children with autism and related disabilities whose purpose it is to prepare children for their future. Throughout the years, I have worked with individuals who have varying disabilities, and one goal has always been to teach skills in a way that is meaningful, purposeful, measurable, doable, and attainable. However, what was lacking was a systematic way of organizing the instruction. There were some variables that stayed the same- for example, using different prompts to ensure the task was completed, providing reinforcement for "jobs well done", and in some settings, collecting data. But there never seemed to be a reliable way of ensuring that a variety of people could teach the same child the same skill and still yield the same result - skill acquisition. I hope that this volume will help achieve this way by using these lesson plans designed to be comprehensive enough to allow "teachers" to reliably teach students. The lesson plans contain critical instructional "elements" that when followed, increase the probability that students will acquire skills in a systematic and functional manner. The elements described within this book are derived from the *Pyramid Approach to Education* (Bondy, 2011)

The plans included within this volume are intended for younger students, but the targeted skills are somewhat ageless. For example, there is not an age limit for learning to brush teeth, dress and undress, or request items from peers. Individuals of all ages benefit from the increased independence that comes from being able to complete these objectives without additional assistance or supervision. The lesson plan format itself enables the "teacher" (i.e., any person in a teaching role relative to children or other learners) to instruct within parameters that are essential to fostering the acquisition of new skills. Many believe that when a student is not acquiring a desired skill, that the student must not be ready to learn; we believe that students are always ready to learn - the better question is - are teachers prepared to teach? With the strategies described in the Pyramid Approach and with the details outlined by these lessons, we hope that teachers are now better equipped to teach.
This manual is for the "teachers"…

Kate Dickey

The Pyramid Approach to Education is a comprehensive set of strategies to help design effective educational environments for children with autism and other moderate and severe disabilities. This Approach rests upon the principles of learning identified within the field of applied behavior analysis. I developed the Pyramid Approach while director of a statewide public school program for students with autism. The model is used as the basis for both staff and parent training. Its application is suitable for settings within schools, as well as domestic and community settings.

The Pyramid Approach is a complex, interactive model that guides teachers in a series of questions about the overall teaching process. The model resembles a physical pyramid, and as such, requires attention to the base of the pyramid before working on issues within the full body of the pyramid. The lessons shared within this Volume are all based upon strategies described in detail *The Pyramid Approach to Education* by Bondy (2011) and are meant to accompany that book. A brief summary of the key aspects of the Pyramid Approach follows this introduction.

The purpose of this book is to provide teachers and others with examples of how to design specific lessons for young children within the Pyramid Approach framework. The design of each lesson depends upon identifying key elements within a lesson, including the long-term goal of the lesson, prompting and error correction strategies, as well as issues pertaining to generalization and reinforcement. There are only a few core lesson formats- one for lessons involving discrete types of learning- whether discrimination, object use, communication, or similar units- one for lessons involving sequential tasks (e.g., brushing teeth, setting a table, etc.), and one for student initiated activities (e.g., requesting reinforcers). A Guideline is provided to help teachers identify and define precisely the type of information appropriate to each box within each data form.

We have focused Volume One on young children. However, we are not suggesting that this volume is a complete set of potential objectives or that these lessons would not be appropriate for older students or adults. We also offer these as examples of how to design effective lessons without suggesting that these are the only ways to teach these lessons. In time, we hope to develop other lesson sets that will help elucidate the variety of effective lessons that can be designed for particular skills. For example, we do not think there is only one way to teach shoe tying or 'going shopping.' There are several ways to effectively tie one's shoes. The skills involved in shopping change as the age and skill level of a student changes, thus leading to variations in the shopping lesson.

We hope you will find these lessons helpful in your effort to teach young children with autism and other disabilities. We understand that at first glance these forms may seem daunting. While they seem to require a great deal of information they were developed over a long period of time by staff working with children with complex learning needs. We found that describing less information would lead to severe problems over time if the initial lesson were not completely successful. That is, if a problem develops for child learning a skill, then it is the teacher who must modify the lesson. Without providing details on all the aspects noted in these lesson plans, adequate alternatives are hard to describe. Therefore, as you read the guidelines, forms, and lesson plans themselves, if you feel there is indeed an area that is not helpful, we hope you will share this with us so that we can improve the format over time. Similarly, if there is a type of information that you think must be included but is not within the current form, we also hope you will contact us with your suggestions.

Andy Bondy

The Pyramid Approach to Education

Andy Bondy[1]

Teaching is a very complex process. It would be wonderful if it were simple and straightforward. Teachers easily would learn a linear model, such as a set of steps on a staircase. However, we know that life is more convoluted and interactive than any linear model could guide us through. A more realistic model for describing the elements necessary to create effective educational environments is portrayed by the Pyramid Approach to Education (see Bondy, 2011). A pyramid is three-dimensional, and has a wide and firm foundation that must be built before the full body of the pyramid can be constructed. What are the critical elements of this approach?

Consider your first experiences working with children (or adults) with autism or other complex disabilities. You most likely recall a child who engaged in a variety of actions that you were not thrilled to see such as hitting, kicking, running around, rearranging furniture and other parts of your classroom or home, screaming, crying, tantruming, hitting or hurting himself or others. At the same time, you most likely noted that many skills were 'missing'- skills such as functional communication, social interactions, appropriate play, turn-taking, and attending to things you thought important. Thus, while you see many behavior excesses that you want to eliminate, you also know that there are many deficits that need to be addressed. Important questions facing a teacher when trying to plan to deal with such a new student include, "Where do I begin? Should I try to get rid of some behaviors or shall I try to teach new ones?"

One traditional approach is to try to get rid of inappropriate or interfering behaviors in hopes of "getting the child ready to learn." However, the implication here is that unless a child is calmly sitting in a chair, with hands in lap, looking at the teacher for several seconds before the instruction is given, no learning is possible. From a behavioral perspective, this is an unusual stance to take as it implies no learning is possible until some almost magical point in time is achieved. We know that children can learn in any situation- though not always the lessons we want to teach. It is true that our jobs as teachers are 'easier' if the child is attentively sitting in a chair, but making a teacher's job easier is not our goal. Our goal in planning to teach our students is determining what we need to do to make lessons more effective. Some children may engage in actions that interfere with attending to the teacher. However, in many cases poorly designed lessons could lead to inappropriate behaviors. Our preference is to design lessons in such a way that the student learns without necessarily resorting to behaviors that are ineffective or inappropriate. Furthermore, as will be made clearer in a moment, before we try to eliminate a behavior (or reduce its frequency or intensity) we must first determine why the behavior is occurring and then replace that particular behavior with one that meets the same goals for the child and yet is more socially acceptable.

The foundation of the Pyramid Approach rests upon the field of Applied Behavior Analysis- the field devoted to the science of learning. The basic premise of Applied Behavior Analysis (ABA) and The Pyramid Approach to Education is that behavior is lawfully related to environmental factors (including those within the individual). If we can understand the process of learning then we will be better prepared to effectively teach new skills.

The Base Elements of the Pyramid

All buildings require a firm foundation and the Pyramid Approach is no different. The base of the Pyramid involves four elements. These elements deal with the broad issues of *"WHAT"* to teach and *"WHY"* students learn. Of course, our concern about Contextually Inappropriate Behaviors is one of the base elements but it is not where we begin our focus.

---

[1] From The Picture Exchange Communication System (PECS) Training Manual, 2nd Edition, Frost & Bondy (2002), Pyramid Educational Consultants: Newark, DE.

Functional Objectives

The first element addressed deals with what we should teach children, or ***Functional Objectives***. Our goal in teaching children with autism and other severe disabilities should be the same as our goal for educating all students- to teach them skills so that when they leave school, they obtain a good job and go live somewhere other than with their parents! We emphasize the importance of remembering that we teach skills such as reading or math not to end up saying, "He can read at a 3rd grade level" but because improved reading or math skills lead to obtaining a better job or living more independently.

Related to this issue of functional objectives is our concern about using functional materials. For example, assume that your current developmental profile on your newest 5-year-old student indicates that she does not know her colors. Upon reading the IEP objective, "Mary will learn her colors," most teachers will attempt to create a color lesson for Mary. A common lesson would be to place a red block and a blue block in front of Mary and then say, "touch red" (or some similar variation on this lesson type). As teachers, we are concerned that this type of lesson is not very thrilling to teach, nor is it very intriguing for students (especially those with autism who may not yet participate in lessons simply to please their teacher). However, in addition to concerns about how motivating this lesson may be is a concern about linking this lesson to other important related skills— how will this skill be used in daily life. We doubt that in Mary's daily life will she be asked or told to touch red or blue blocks!

For example, after lunch, you have Mary brush her teeth. To accomplish this task, she must go into the bathroom and find her toothbrush from among the 8 brushes of her classmates. Most likely, she will need to 'know the color' of her toothbrush. Will months of sitting at a table doing the 'point to red' block lesson automatically transfer to or generalize to the toothbrushes in the bathroom? Unfortunately, practical experience has shown that this transfer does not readily occur. For many children, teachers find themselves teaching the color lesson again in the bathroom with the toothbrushes. We know that teaching Mary to brush her teeth is an important and functional skill. We cannot say the same for touching colored blocks. However, is there any evidence that teaching a student 'colors' with blocks is more effective than using toothbrushes? The simple answer is, "no!" The question is, why do so many of us start the lesson with blocks? Regrettably, the most likely answer is that it is easier to use the blocks than the toothbrushes. We believe that spending time gathering functional materials (in this case, many items involving color that are important to Mary) will more than pay off in the reduction in time for the student to truly acquire the skill being taught.

Powerful Reinforcement Systems

The second core element of the base of the Pyramid involves the use of ***Powerful Reinforcement Systems***. One of the issues addressed in this area involves the recognition that students define what is rewarding to them, not teachers. Related to this emphasis is our awareness that we may not like all the reinforcers that are effective for a student! However, while we should work toward developing new sources of motivation for a student (similar to when you or I took an art-appreciation class) such changes will take some time. Until those new reinforcers are effective, we must use what is immediately available (unless, of course, it involves things that are dangerous to the student or others).

We emphasize using reinforcers for completing actions that are as 'natural' to the situation as possible. For example, a natural consequence for putting on sneakers is getting to run around outside. To start a lesson involving learning to lace up sneakers, we use a "reinforcer first" strategy. That is, *first* we would let the student know about the available reinforcer. For example, while Phoebe is running about inside the room without any shoes on, we say, "Phoebe, let's go outside!" Then, when Phoebe starts to head for the door, we would then say, "Oh, we need our sneakers on to go outside!" In this manner, when Phoebe does lace her sneakers, her reward is going outside (rather than some arbitrary reward such as a piece of candy).

Of course, we also must note that while the consequences for completing a task should be as natural as possible, many activities will require rewards while the skill is being accomplished. In our example, while Phoebe is lacing her sneakers- a complex sequence of actions- we may provide small rewards such as praise or even provide some tokens to help her understand how long this task will last. Such small rewards are identified as within-task reinforcers.

Another central issue regarding the use of reinforcement concerns the timing of providing the reward. We all know that rewards should come quickly after our target skill. However, we want to operationalize 'quickly' by noting that reinforcers that are delayed by more than ½ a second reduce the power of the reinforcer! Whenever a new skill is to be learned, including the steps within PECS, teachers must determine ways to provide positive feedback within ½ second of that new skill!

Related to the speed of providing reinforcers are factors associated with the differential use of reinforcement. That is, we can reward one behavior but not another or we may reinforce one behavior more than another. In the latter case, each response is followed by reinforcement but one response will be favored because it is connected to more reinforcement. In this way, we can remain positive while teaching, "This response is better than that one!"

Essential to the Pyramid Approach is how we interact with our students. We believe that we should engage in "Let's Make a Deal" with our students. Why make deals with students? Well, teachers expect their students to learn. Learning involves changing behaviors- that is, after a lesson, students should do something that they couldn't do before the lesson (i.e., say something, use a new picture, button a coat, recite the Gettysburg Address, etc.). Thus, teachers want students to do something (learn) for them! The relationship between teacher and student is thus similar to the relationship between a boss and a worker- the boss expects the worker to do something (the job) for the boss! When we work with students, we are "the boss." However, as teachers in a school, we all work for someone- our own bosses. As workers, we have certain expectations about our relationship with our boss that we believe are equally important to establish in our relationship with our student. If I don't know what I'm going to get paid for a job, I won't start the job. With students, we adopt a similar simple rule- no reinforcer, no lesson!

For example, before we start a job, we want to know what we will get paid, when we get paid, how many vacation days we'll get, and other important factors. Furthermore, even though we have excellent verbal skills (and I'll assume so does your boss!), we want a written contract specifying our deal with the boss- that is, we insist on having a visual representation of the deal. We believe that issues that are important or valued by us should be in place for our students. That is, they too deserve to know what their potential reinforcer is before the lesson starts (i.e., reinforcer first!), when they will receive their reinforcer, and how they will get a break during a lesson. They also should have a visual representation of their deal with us! While this may sound like a mighty large order, by the end of this manual, you will see how simply we can accomplish this goal.

Communication and Social Skills

The next element of the Pyramid involves functional *Communication and Social Skills*. Communication involves certain types of interactions between people. We define *functional communication* as:

> Behavior (defined in form by the community) directed to another person who in turn
> provides related direct or social rewards.

In this definition we describe the interaction between a 'speaker' and a 'listener' -regardless of whether speech is used. If there is no 'listener' then the action- even if it does involve vocal noises- may not be communicative.

We recognize that there are two broad reasons or functions for communicating with someone. In some circumstances, we make a request or demand something. I may ask for some juice or for you to go away. The outcome or consequence for this type of communication involves direct reinforcement. On the other hand, at times, upon seeing something interesting, a child may name the object or event not as a request for the item but to engage someone in a simple conversation (such as when Mom says, "Yes, it is a pretty rose!"). Here, the outcome is social in nature. When we are working with young children with autism, we notice that they tend not to be highly motivated by social rewards. Therefore, the type of communication lesson we choose should be related to the types of reinforcers that will be effective for a student.

In addition to noting the type of consequence for communicating, it also is important to note the conditions or circumstances under which communication takes place. At times, upon seeing someone with a cookie, a boy may spontaneously say, "cookie!" At other times, the child may say, "cookie" only when someone says, "What do you want?" or "What do you see?" Finally, a child may say, "cookie" only when someone models the word and prompts the child to imitate. In each of these three situations, the child says the word "cookie." While the form is the same, each response is really a different behavior. That is, initiating is not the same as responding to a prompt or imitating. These three types of behavior initially are acquired independently (for all children, not just children with disabilities). That is, early in language development, if one type of behavior is learned (i.e., imitating a spoken word) the other types of use- initiation or responding to prompts- may not automatically appear (i.e., generalization across these response classes may not occur). Over time and experience, we see generalization readily occur but until that happens, we must plan to teach each skill individually.

Communication is bi-directional. While we may focus a great deal of attention on improving children's ability to use communication, we also want children to understand our communication to them. Here again, the transfer from using communication to understanding others' communication is not automatic early in language development. A child may understand a word but not be able to use it, and a child may also learn to say a word without seeming to understand it when spoken by others.

In our society, speech is the most common mode of communication and obviously the most preferred. However, even those of us who speak use other forms to enhance the effectiveness of what we're saying- we alter our facial expressions, our body movements, our intonation and inflections. Gestures can be formalized into sign language. Furthermore, we use print media to read and write and understand a host of visual signs and cues in the environment (traffic lights, painted lines on the road, arrows, etc.). Is the use of these other modalities dependent upon prior speech development? Certainly not, as we all know that some people learn to sign or even read and write without ever developing speech. Thus, when we note that someone cannot communicate, there are several options to choose from regarding the modality to be taught.

Preventing and Reducing Contextually Inappropriate Behaviors

The final element of base of the Pyramid concerns *Preventing and Reducing Contextually Inappropriate Behaviors*. In this area, we make an important distinction between the form the behavior takes vs. *why* the behavior occurs— the function. Furthermore, the development of effective interventions depends upon a clear understanding of the function of the behavior in question. Three broad types of functions are identified:

1. Behaviors that **gain access** to some type of reinforcement (including attention, materials, sensory stimulation or activities)
2. Behaviors that **escape from or avoid** certain outcomes (including social, activity, or material consequences)
3. Behaviors that are **elicited** by certain events, including the removal or sharp reduction of expected rewards, presence of pain or similar events, or the introduction of powerful rewards

Effective intervention involves identifying the function of the CIB and then assuring that a functionally equivalent alternative behavior (FEAB) will be supported. That is, if a child is hitting her head to gain attention, then the child must be taught to calmly request attention. If a child is hitting her head to avoid doing a task, then the child may need to learn to request help or to request a break. If the child is hitting her head because someone has just told her that it's raining so she can't go outside just now, then she needs to learn how to wait. Note that the replacement must serve the same function as the CIB.

Many effective prevention strategies have been developed involving altering conditions that tend to precede a CIB. Successful interventions also involve planned direct reactions when the CIB does occur and implementing strategies to reward the absence of the CIB or the presence of the alternatives noted above.

The Top Elements of the Pyramid

The upper portion of this model deals with issues of *how* to teach effective lessons. Before we begin teaching the lesson, we develop a plan for generalization of the new skill. We design effective lessons using a teaching strategy that is specific to the type of skill being taught. Before beginning to teach, we anticipate what type of errors the student might make and develop a plan for responding to those errors.

Generalization

When planning to teach a new skill, we must know how that skill will help the student gain more independence, either immediately or in the future. In other words, we must know "where we're going" with this skill. Is this skill one that will be used as a "stepping stone" for the next skill we teach? Is this skill one that we are teaching after simplifying a broader skill? One unique aspect of the Pyramid model is our emphasis on addressing generalization from the very start of a lesson. That is, rather than working toward skill mastery and then planning for generalization, we think it is important to know where a lesson is going even before beginning.

Many strategies have been designed to promote generalization from early in a lesson. Most of these strategies involve making gradual, small changes that accumulate over time to result in substantial behavior improvements. The key is to make changes that are large enough for the teacher to know a change has been made but small enough that the student doesn't seem to notice the difference. Making such changes within a teaching session is central to the overall model.

These changes are twofold: First, we can make changes in "stimulus" factors. Stimulus factors include issues related to the "other" people involved in the skill– e.g., Can the student engage in the behavior without close supervision and can he engage in the behavior when in a crowded situation? Stimulus factors involve the places where the behavior will occur– fix a sandwich in a variety of kitchens. Can the student engage in the behavior at various times of day (e.g., can he ask for a drink whenever he is thirsty or only at snack?). Stimulus factors involve the types of materials used in conjunction with the new skill. For example, can the student identify or find the red cup, *and* the red toothbrush, *and* the red coat, *and* the red chair? We look at a variety of environmental factors— can the student greet others when they walk into the room *and* when he walks into a room?

Second, we look for changes in student response factors such as number, rate, duration, complexity, accuracy, durability, and fluency of responses. For example, you have taught your student to help in the school office by sorting teachers' mail into their boxes. You must look at response factors, though, before you consider the skill to be "mastered." Can he sort one envelope or can he sort a whole stack of envelopes? Can he sort quickly and do so for an extended period of time? Can he sort the mail for all of the teachers whose names begin with 's'? Is he accurate when he sorts the materials? Although he can sort the mail for 20 minutes at a time, can he do so 5 days in a row?

Designing Effective Lessons

When planning to teach a skill, we next consider factors associated with *Designing Effective Lessons*. Specific skills are taught best within specific types of lessons. When deciding on a lesson type, we look at whether the lesson will involve:

Relatively direct instructions and simple responses that are teacher-initiated. If so then we use a ***discrete trial*** format.
Examples:
   "What's your name?"
   "Draw a line from A to B."
   "Get me the square cracker."

Skills that require a series of distinct smaller responses put together in a particular order and that generally are teacher initiated. If so, then we use a ***sequential*** format.
Examples:
   Washing hands
   Completing an art project
   Putting away silverware

Child-initiated actions that are in response to naturally occurring cues from the physical (things) or social (people) environment. In this case, we use a student-initiated lesson format (including incidental lessons).

Examples:
   Asking for a drink when thirsty
   Greeting a friend upon seeing her
   Commenting on a loud, sudden sound

Because students ultimately must learn each type of lesson, teachers should develop effective teaching strategies to fit each lesson type. These factors will need to be integrated with other elements of the Pyramid Approach, such as issues associated with emphasizing functional objectives. For example, some lessons may lend themselves to rapid repetition while, for other lessons, immediate repetition would not be natural. If a student is learning to put soap in the dishwasher, it would not make sense to have him repeat this action many times in rapid succession, so we would want to disperse opportunities across the day or across several days. Or if a student is learning to put on a shirt, we would want him to do it at appropriate times. Perhaps before going to gym we would have him change a shirt. It would not make sense for us to have him put on a shirt, take it off, put it on, take it off… because this is not a sequence he's likely to encounter in the "real world."

On the other hand, if a student is doing addition problems, it would make sense to have him do several in a row rather than one per day. Or, if a student is emptying the dishwasher we would want him to sort several utensils into the utensil drawer, not just one each time he unloads the dishwasher.

Specific Teaching Strategies

As we make our detailed lesson plans, we must consider *Specific Teaching Strategies*. Most lessons involve a teacher initially helping a student perform a skill. The type of help we provide involves various *prompts*, including verbal, gestural, modeling, and physical prompts. The key to a successful lesson is that it results in a student being able to perform the skill independently of our assistance- therefore, our goal is to eliminate the prompts used to help the student. Once we've eliminated the prompts, the skill then occurs in response to natural cues in the environment, whether physical, social, or internal. These cues are identified as discriminative stimuli because they now have *stimulus control* over the new skill. For example, if we are working with a student who can imitate words, we may hold up an apple and model the word. When the child says, 'apple' he is imitating our actions. Later, when we can only hold up the apple and the child says, 'apple' the stimulus control has shifted from our modeled word to the physical apple.

We differentiate *prompts* from *cues*. The student engages in a behavior in response to a *prompt* that we must eliminate. He engages in a behavior in response to cues that we will not eliminate. For example, in a high school, students arriving at school know to report to their first class in response to a bell ringing. Some students also need us to verbally remind them ("Go to class!"). Our verbal reminder is the prompt that we hope to fade over time while the cue is a signal that we do not intend to fade. Within this differentiation, imagine viewing a stop sign as a prompt vs. a cue. Do we ever intend to fade the stop sign—do we really expect *all* drivers to learn over time at which corners they must stop? Certainly not! Thus, the stop sign is viewed as a cue, not a prompt. Now, if you are a parent with a teen-aged child learning to drive, you might have to *prompt* your child to stop at a stop sign ("There's a stop sign—stop!!"). We would not let our child drive alone, however, until he learned to respond to the cue (the stop sign) and did not need our additional prompt.

There are a variety of prompting strategies designed to eliminate the prompt while leaving the performance under the control of natural conditions (cues). These strategies include fading, prompt hierarchies (whether most-to-least or least-to-most, delayed prompting (both constant and progressive), and using chaining strategies (both forward and backward chaining).

Shaping is an important teaching technique. In its pure form, it does not involve the use of prompts. Instead, shaping involves the gradual change in the criteria we set for reinforcement. We feel that shaping is an underutilized teaching tool in large part because it does not involve the types of active prompting that so many of us are comfortable using within a lesson.

Minimizing and Correcting Errors

The most effective lessons are those that involve few mistakes by the student. Of course, it is virtually impossible to prevent all errors. Therefore, the next element involves *Minimizing and Correcting Errors*. Lessons that involve a series of small, gradual changes tend to minimize errors and thus maximize a student's receipt of reinforcement. When errors do occur, we must be aware of the type of lesson we are teaching before deciding what type of correction strategy we want. A correction strategy aims to teach the skill immediately rather than simply fixing the problem caused by the error. For example, if a student fails to tie his shoe properly, I may tie it for him- thus fixing the problem- but the student will have not learned anything new (other than I am likely to solve his problems!).

4-Step Error Correction Procedure. When lessons involve discrete trial formats, we respond with a **4-step** error correction process. First, we will need to model, demonstrate or otherwise indicate the correct response. Then, we need to help the student engage in the correct action. However, at this point we may not want to provide a big type of reward lest the student become dependent upon the prompt just provided. Instead, we suggest switching to another task, one that is simple, quick, and mastered by the student. (If there are few such available actions, a delay of some sort may be equally effective.) Then we would repeat the initial part of the lesson and provide a strong reinforcer for a successful response.

For example, during morning circle in a preschool class, the teacher asks, "What day is it?" Mike incorrectly answers, "Tuesday." The teacher says, 'No, it's Wednesday." Mike repeats, "Wednesday." The teacher responds, "Yes!" In this scenario, Mike said the correct word, but he said it by imitating the teacher rather than answering the question. If the teacher were to stop at this point, all Mike would have learned is to repeat the teacher's answers. Minimally, the teacher needs to ask the question again. When she does so and Mike answers, "Wednesday," we are a bit more confident that Mike is learning the lesson. But, many children, with and without disabilities, adopt a "whatever was right last time" strategy. In order to undermine the potential for Mike to use this strategy, the teacher should ask Mike something completely unrelated, but that he can answer, and then re-ask the original question. This time, when Mike answers, "Wednesday," he is doing it solely in response to the question rather than in response to a teacher model or his own last response.

Backstep Error Correction Procedure. Errors that occur within a sequential lesson require different correction strategies. In such situations, it is important to note that we often find the error long after it was made. That is, the error is likely to have occurred sometime earlier in the sequence than when we discovered it. In this case, we must help the student go back into the sequence just prior to when the error occurred. Following this type of **Backstep**, we would prompt the correct action in its proper place in the sequence. If we prompt the student from the point where we found the error- the student is in my classroom but he left the water running in the bathroom so I tell him to go turn it off- then I am likely to see that error preserved and repeated on the next opportunity. Once we prompt the student within the Backstep sequence, we then differentially reinforce the completion of the sequence but giving a reward that is effective, but not as powerful as one we would use for independent completion of the sequence.

Anticipatory Prompting. In some cases, it may not be possible to immediately go back into the sequence. For example, if we are attempting to teach someone to ride on a public bus and she forgets to pay the bus driver, we will not be able to stop the bus, get off it, and try again. Instead, we must **anticipate** the error on the next natural opportunity and provide a prompt that prevents its repetition (and then fade that prompt over time).

Collecting and Analyzing Data

Central to a behavioral or education model is making decisions based upon evaluating what we've done. A core question every teacher must ask about every lesson is, "Is this a good lesson? Shall I keep doing what I've been doing?" Answering this question involves collecting information about the teacher's actions as well as the student's performance. Useful information also may be derived from other sources, including other staff, parents, and peers of the student. To be useful, the data must be gathered and summarized in a manner that permits periodic analysis.

Data collection and analysis can be effortful and time consuming. Thus, the process requires various types of reinforcement. Perhaps the most important rewarding consequence of collecting and analyzing data is having the data help refine a lesson. If the data are not used in a meaningful manner, we tend not to continue collecting it as a way of avoiding wasting our time. While percent-correct may fit some lessons, progress in other lessons may better involve rate, duration, intensity, accuracy, prompt-level, etc. How much data is required, how often should it be reviewed, and what type of potential changes should be made related to our findings, all should be decided upon by the student's full team (rather than individual members of the team).

The type of data collected should reflect the broad range of factors that may be important within different lessons. In some situations, the frequency and rate of an action are most important. In other cases, the duration, intensity, complexity, or accuracy may be focal point of a lesson. Finally, we may observe behavior as it occurs or we may evaluate the product of the lesson (i.e., a clean room, a neatly printed letter, a sentence strip with 3 icons in the correct order within PECS, etc.).

Linking the Elements of the Pyramid

The Pyramid Approach involves a complex model of factors required to make lessons as effective as possible in various environments. The order in which the model has been presented here also is the order in which we support teachers in making changes to implement the full model. That is, it is important to first assure that powerful reinforcement systems are in place before attempting to refine subtle aspects of prompting or error correction. Teaching critical functional communication skills is crucial even before the development of significant behavior management plans for a student. In classrooms and other teaching environments that use The Pyramid Approach to Education, many of the critical aspects noted are prominently posted so that all members of the team are equally aware of the critical information regarding a student.

The elements of lessons involving PECS are very much like any other lesson. First, a reinforcer associated with the skill to be learned must be identified and its availability made clear to the student. We must determine the type of lesson that leads into a review of potential prompting or shaping strategies. We must anticipate the type of error that can occur within this type of lesson and plan for the corresponding error correction strategy. We must assure that we provide timely reinforcement in amounts that lead to skill growth and long-term independence. We must collect adequate data to justify our current strategies or to help suggest alternative teaching strategies. If inappropriate behaviors occur, we must have a system in place to help determine the function of the behavior, how to respond to the behavior, how to help prevent the behavior, and how to promote functionally equivalent alternative behaviors.

All of these steps require strong and continuous staff and parent training and support. Without adequately trained teachers, we cannot expect students to progress. The Pyramid Approach offers teachers and parents a problem-solving orientation by which they can design and analyze effective lessons, including those for our most complex students.

Lesson Formats

How do we teach effectively? We use lesson formats to organize the 'hows' and 'whats' of teaching a particular skill. Before you sit down and design the actual lesson you will first need to review the child's current IEP objectives so that you can match the individual goals with the lesson format that best facilitates learning. It is important to systematically outline the various elements of the lesson plan prior to working on the target skill with the child. These elements include: specific behavioral objective, distribution of reinforcement, prompting strategies, error correction strategies, generalization techniques, functional activities in which to incorporate the lesson, as well as needed materials for instruction. Some objectives, such as teaching requesting food items during snack, occur naturally and daily in the classroom, while other skills, such as teaching name-writing or collating office materials, need to be carefully arranged in order for teaching opportunities to occur. There are advantages and disadvantages associated with each lesson format and it is the responsibility of the team to choose the best strategy for each lesson.

The following is a description of several types of lesson format categories broken down into further categories based on the particular area of teaching/emphasis:

Discrete trial lesson formats typically involve direct instructions and simple responses. A discrete trial is an interactive progression that involves a clear, succinct, and discriminable antecedent (i.e., the discriminative stimulus), a behavioral response, and a relatively simple consequence followed by a brief pause. The consequence can either be positive reinforcement or instructional feedback (Koegel, Russo, & Rincover, 1977[2]). The lesson is usually initiated by the teacher issuing an instruction, and the responses given by the student are simple and direct. Discrete trial lessons typically occur in small repeatable steps that allows for the repetition of stimulus and responses. This format is commonly used when the objective deals with actions that can stand-alone and are not linked to other actions/behaviors. This format is also useful when staff wish to have many repetitions of an action in a short period of time. For example, various discrimination lessons (e.g., big vs. little, shapes, numbers, colors, yes/no, etc.) may involve this type of instructional format because it allows for relatively rapid repetition of the skill. However, because of the circumstances under which discrete trial is often implemented and the prepared materials, it is very important to plan from the start for generalization of the lesson and skill to more natural contexts. It should also be recognized that not every discrete trial lesson lends itself to rapid repetition. For example, if a student replied "yes" to "Do you want to go outside?" we should not repeat the question a set number of times- rather, we should let the child go outside.

Sequential lessons involve small, individual steps that occur in a specific order, and when put all together form a larger skill. These lesson formats also typically are teacher initiated. The teacher is in charge of directing the sequence of the target skill and providing systematic instruction at the individual step level. For example, turning off the water is one distinctive step in the sequence of the larger skill of washing your hands. Once you have determined that the skills you are going to be teaching in a sequential lesson, you need to answer the following questions. Is the skill going to be presented in its entirety (**whole task**)? Or is only part of the sequence going to be targeted (**partial task**)? Once these questions have been answered, it is time to determine the specific steps that

---

[2] Koegel, R.L., Russo, D.C., & Rincover, A. (1977). Assessing and training the generalized use of behavior modification with autistic children. *Journal of Applied Behavior Analysis, 10,* 197-205.

comprise the sequence - the task analysis. Once the steps have been determined, a decision must be made regarding instructing the sequence from the beginning (**forward**) or from the end (**backward**). Below are further definitions and distinctions:

Whole task, also known as **total task,** refers to the entire task being presented in sequence, from start to end. Typically, some type of prompting is used throughout to assure student participation. This strategy is most often used in community settings, and with many domestic and vocational objectives. In these settings, it is not feasible to repeat a portion of the task even if an error has been made.

Partial task refers to a segment (just part of the sequence) of the lesson being presented. For example, during an arts and crafts activity, staff may decide to cut out the shapes (e.g., animals) that are going to be pasted on the project and have the students simply focus on the pasting the cut-outs. Another example is one in which you are teaching the student to set the table and have all the needed materials set out rather than also teaching the child to obtain all the necessary materials and then set the table. Obtaining the materials can be taught secondary to the child acquiring the skill of setting the table.

A **task analysis** involves the identification of a series of independent steps that make up a complete activity. A task analysis is not a lesson format but is necessary for other lesson formats and prompt strategies to be completed. For example, tooth brushing, getting dressed, washing hands, and food preparation are examples of tasks that require multiple steps be completed in order for the task itself to be complete. A task analysis provides a list of each step that is involved in the completion of the task, in its proper sequence. Because each student is unique and skill acquisition differs, there are no universal task analyses. However, as there will be some similarities across students and tasks, we encourage staff to share their task analyses. Therefore, it is suggested that a file of completed task analysis be made available to all staff. For many types of lessons, the rate of responding is usually noted (e.g., discrete trial) but with a task analysis data often addresses the degree of prompt independence versus prompt level (e.g., verbal, gestural, model, physical).

Forward and Backward Chains refer to which end of the task analysis will be taught first. *Forward* chains involve starting a lesson with the first step of the sequence and then providing the necessary support for the remainder of the steps through completion. Forward chains are typically used if the target skill is not a new one or if the child already can complete some of the steps of the task analysis independently. A *backward* chain refers to prompting or supporting a student through the beginning of the task and then starting instruction on the last step of the sequence. As the child correctly and independently completes a step, then the previous step is added to the sequence until the series is complete. Basically, you are working from the end of the sequence to the beginning in terms of acquiring independence. This is especially helpful if it is a new skill for the student and/or if accessing reinforcement needs to be immediate. Because the student has completed the last step of the sequence they are immediately reinforced versus having to complete multiple steps of the sequence and then gain access to reinforcement.

Student initiated/Incidental lessons are activities/actions that are initiated by the child but then expanded upon by the teacher. For example, the student goes over to the play area and independently sits down and is playing with the toy farm and animals. The teacher can then go over and sit with the child, expanding the play situation to include names of animals, animal sounds, imitation of animal actions, etc. Incidental lessons follow the student's lead. This type of lesson is facilitated within naturally occurring contexts and is usually student led or initiated. This type of format is also described as taking advantage of the teaching opportunity as it is presented versus creating for the teaching opportunity. Teaching incidental lessons is generally more flexible than discrete trial formats but may be more difficult to assess. For example, while playing with crayons with a student, the teacher may try to emphasize talking about colors, shapes, different types of lines, without indicating how many of each condition must occur during the lesson.

Prompt Strategies

Now that you have determined the form the lesson is going to take (discrete, sequential, incidental), it is time to determine the appropriate instructional strategy. Prompting is one of the most powerful instructional techniques that we use. The purpose of the prompt is to help the desired outcome - skill acquisition. However, it can be confusing trying to decide which prompting strategy will guarantee this outcome. So let's begin by defining what a prompt actually is: it is a stimulus that is temporarily provided to the natural context/situation to help the student perform the skill. Prompts can take a variety of forms and before we discuss these in detail, we first need to discuss the difference between a prompt and a cue. We should decide **before** we begin instruction what the long-term cue to this behavior is going to be. That is, once the child has acquired the skill, what is going to occur in the environment that will cue this behavior to happen? For example, when teaching a child to tie his shoes, what will naturally occur that will indicate to the child that he needs to tie his shoes? That's right, his shoes will be untied. Let's look at another example; if we are teaching a child to wash her hands, what will eventually be the natural cue(s) to perform this task? Right again, her hands are dirty, after toileting, and before meals should trigger this desired response. These are the natural cues that direct the behavior. Natural cues remain part of the environment and will not be removed over time. It is very important to note that it is okay - sometimes necessary - to introduce prompts in order to successfully instruct a child in a particular skill area. However, it is crucial that we have a plan to remove all prompts. Since we are striving for children to perform skills autonomously to help them lead independent and productive lives, then their performance must occur in the absence of prompts, (e.g., help). Again, we need to determine what the long-term natural cue will be before we begin any type of instruction, so that we can strive toward that cue being the trigger for the desired behavior and not our prompts.

When selecting the appropriate prompt keep the following guidelines in mind: ultimately, use prompts that work; use prompts that are as close to the natural cues as possible; model or demonstrate to the student the desired response; and use prompts that will be the easiest to gradually remove and fade out completely. There are a limited number of prompting strategies available, so as you become more familiar with them, the lessons, and your students, the task of determining the correct strategy for each lesson will become much easier. The following outlines provide descriptions of each prompting strategy and the appropriate lesson forms associated with each strategy.

Prompt Hierarchy

A prompt hierarchy involves selecting a series of prompts and systematically applying them to instruction. Prompt hierarchies can include full physical prompts, in which the teacher fully assists the child in performing the desired objective by physically managing the student. For example, if the student is learning to follow the direction, "Close the door" then the teacher would give the direction and then physically help the student close the door by putting her hands on the student's hands or by physically moving the child's arms so that they then push the door closed. A less intrusive prompt is the partial physical prompt. This is similar to the previous prompt but the teacher provides less physical intervention in order for the student to accomplish the objective. In the same scenario, the teacher may only need to gently guide the student's arm to the door by gently nudging under the elbow, which results in the desired effect- the door is closed. Another type of prompt, modeling, involves the teacher performing or demonstrating the desired response for the student to imitate. It is important to note that children with autism do not necessarily possess the ability to imitate actions. In such cases, modeling would not be the best prompt to utilize in obtaining the desired response. In our example, the teacher could close the door as a model of the action for the student to imitate. A less intense type of prompt involves the use of a gesture. A gestural prompt signals the target response and can include a point, a tap, or a look in the direction of the desired response or associated object. In our example, the teacher might provide the direction, "Close the door", and then *point* to the open door. One additional type of prompt level is a verbal prompt involving the provision of vocal instructions. Because it is mentioned last, one may think that this would signify that it is the least intrusive prompt; in actuality, it can be the most difficult of all the prompts to eliminate, so use them sparingly and wisely.

A few noteworthy items to mention about prompt hierarchies. First, they can be extremely effective if used correctly. For instance, each prompt should only be used once before moving to the next in the sequence. It is important to allow the student enough time to respond to the current prompt before introducing another. This response time is called the *pause interval* and is the time that is provided between prompt levels. Second, the prompt hierarchy can be presented in one of two ways. First, there is the *least to most* prompt hierarchy, in which the least intrusive prompt is given first and the teacher systematically provides the other prompts in the sequence until the desired response is given by the student. Using a least to most hierarchy is most effective if the student already knows part of the target response. The other way that a prompt hierarchy can be presented is in the *most to least* format, in which the most intrusive prompt is given first and yields the desired response. This type is most effective in teaching new skills to students because it immediately helps the student perform the desired response since you are physically prompting it. You will need to adjust/create the most effective prompt hierarchy for each student and each lesson. For example, a student may like to be physically prompted so in designing an effective prompt hierarchy for her you may eliminate the physical prompt all together. And as previously mentioned you may also eliminate modeled prompts if you know that the student does not have the ability to imitate responses. In other words, tailor the hierarchies to best suit the individual needs of the student and to ensure the most effective means of skill acquisition. In most instances, prompt hierarchies are instituted during sequential lessons.

Delayed Prompting

This type of strategy can be further defined as either *progressive time delay* or *constant time delay*. Let's discuss progressive time delay first. The way that delayed prompting works is that the teacher provides the task direction/cue and the prompt that will guarantee the desired response simultaneously. The prompt that ensures the target response is called the *controlling prompt* because it controls the response. The controlling prompt will differ per individual but in most cases will be either a physical or gestural prompt. But keep in mind that delayed prompting will only work if a controlling prompt has been identified. There are instances in which a student has yet not shown consistent response patterns to a particular prompt, and in these cases a delayed prompting strategy would not work because you could not count on the student responding correctly to the prompt being provided. The teacher will want to use the least intrusive prompt, but the one that does guarantee the desired response. By instructing this way, the student is unable to make a mistake, in fact, the teacher is prompting the desired response from the start of instruction. Over time, the teacher will gradually and systematically increase the time between providing the task direction and the prompt (controlling prompt) that will guarantee the desired response. The time increase occurs in intervals of seconds (e.g., 0, 1, 2, 3, 4, 5). So one proceeds from 0 time delay - meaning there is not a delay between providing the task direction and the prompt - to 1 second which means that the teacher will provide the task direction and then count 1 (silently to themselves) and then provide the prompt that will ensure the correct response, to counting 2 seconds before providing the prompt, to counting 3 before providing the prompt, etc. Usually, at around 2 to 4 seconds is when the student begins to provide the desired response in the absence of the teacher needing to provide the prompt. This is called "beating the prompt" and this is exactly what we want. The student is now responding correctly and in the absence of prompts to the task direction. A constant time delay refers to one in which the time between providing the task direction and the prompt remains the same throughout the lesson.

Model/Demonstration

This instructional strategy involves showing/demonstrating to the student what the desired response is. The target response can either be one step/action or consist of multiple steps/actions, but either way the student must demonstrate prior skill in imitating the actions of others if this strategy is to be effective. Systematically over time, the teacher provides less and less demonstration of the target response and the student continues to engage in the entire response.

Shaping

This strategy involves gradually increasing the criteria needed for reinforcement of the desired response. In other words, the prompts that you are providing remain the same; it is the level of response/performance from the student that changes/increases. The changes should be subtle to the student and noticeable to the teacher. For example, your student runs down the hallway whenever the classroom door opens. You might mark with tape 1 foot down the hall from the door and upon opening the door the student then has to walk that one foot before being reinforced and then can run the rest of the way. Next you mark off 2 feet and the student has to walk the two feet before being reinforced and then can run the rest of the way, until you have marked off the entire length of the hall and the student is successfully walking. Notice that NO prompts are used in a pure shaping lesson - only the criteria of the response - the distance the student had to walk in order to earn reinforcement - changed subtly over time.

Fading

Fading refers to changing the intensity of the prompt you are providing over time. The prompt given is the same type of prompt - it just differs in intensity provided over time. Fading may include a particular strategy known as graduated guidance. An example of graduated guidance would be if you are trying to teach a student to write her name: you begin by using hand over hand physical assistance (you literally put your hand over top of the student's) and physically prompt the writing. Over time, you fade the prompt to hand on wrist which continues to yield the same result, to hand on forearm, to hand on elbow, to hand on shoulder. Here you provide the same type of prompt - physical - but reduce the intensity, and the target of the physical prompt. The term fading refers to reducing the strength of a particular prompt and other types of prompts are not introduced. Any type of prompt (e.g., verbal, gestural, physical) can be faded.

Error Correction

While working with a student to sort silverware, I notice she keeps putting the spoons in with the forks- what should I do? I'll tell you what I used to do- I took the spoons out and put them where they belong, with the rest of the spoons. Is this correct? NO, and I'll tell you why. Rather than just fix the mistake we need to correct it. There is a difference here. We all have a tendency to fix things; if they are not right then I'll make it right by fixing it-, like putting the spoon where it belongs. We can fix this because we recognize the problem or error. Is the same true for our student? What do they learn when we fix things for them? Do they know that they have made a mistake? Most likely not. Instead of simply fixing the problem we should try to teach the student the correct way of performing the task in the absence of mistakes, and use the error as an additional teaching opportunity. An important teaching rule is to minimize errors from occurring in the first place. But despite our best laid plans, errors will occur - it is how we handle these errors that is important. Therefore, the lessons we develop include a section on error correction so we have a plan in place from the start. Different teaching strategies will require different error correction strategies.

4 - STEP:

While working with a student, you hold up an orange and ask, "What's this?" He answers, "banana." What should you do? First, recognize that this is a type of discrete-trial lesson. We will use a 4-step process to fully respond to this type of error. First, this procedure involves *modeling/demonstrating* to the student what the correct response is- in this case, by saying, "orange." We would then *prompt* the student to make the correct response by using whatever prompt is necessary to have the student 'practice' this correct response. In our example, we know the student is a good imitator and is thus likely to repeat the word "orange" when we immediately say, "What's this?" However, because we just provided an imitative prompt, we will not provide any major reinforcement- that will be reserved for independent responses. We will use differential reinforcement, meaning we will provide a bigger reinforcer for independent responses then for prompted responses. The next step involves distracting the student away from the fact that we just prompted the correct response. We would *switch* to something that the student already knew how to do, often something unrelated to the current task. Some examples of switches include, but certainly are not limited to, the following: we might instruct, "Touch your head", "Clap your hands", "Draw a line", and have them respond to a well-known question. If the student is not yet under good instructional control by even simple tasks, then we might simply insert a pause. Whatever the switch involves, it needs to be something that the student can do independently and something not currently being taught. It will also be very important to change the type of switches so that the student does not learn these responses as part of the error correction sequence. Finally, we will *repeat* the trial and reward successful actions. If the student were to make another error then we repeat the error correction procedure (4-step) once more. If the student makes yet another error then we can elect to repeat the error correction procedure one final time, while simplifying the trial so the student will make the correct response, or simply end the trial/lesson. The rule here is to repeat the error correction procedure a maximum of 2-3 times consecutively. As a direct result of the errors, the student is no longer gaining access to reinforcement. The student is most likely becoming increasingly frustrated and so is the teacher! Thus, end the lesson before an outburst takes place and then refine the lesson before starting up again. Another example of 4-step would be the following: A student is learning to identify body parts within a game that involves placing a sticker on the named body part. When the teacher instructs the student to put the sticker on her nose, she places the sticker on her lips - and an error has occurred. The teacher then quietly says, "No" and *models* putting the sticker on the nose. The teacher then uses the task direction, "Put sticker on nose" while *prompting* the student to put the sticker on her nose (remember use only labeled praise because it was a prompted correct response). Then the teacher *switches* tasks by saying, "Point to the ceiling" and the student momentarily looks up. Then the teacher *repeats* the trial, "Put sticker on your nose." When the student correctly places the sticker on her nose, reinforcement is quickly provided. In terms of data collection, note that the trial was entered as an error (" – ") and no data were collected within the error-correction sequence as this was all part of the single trial.

BACKSTEP:

Another type of lesson that requires a unique error correction strategy involves sequential tasks. When an error occurs within this type of lesson, it is critical to know during which part of the sequence the error has occurred. Our basic strategy will involve going back to that step to ensure that the student has learned the proper sequence.

Pyramid Educational Consultants

Hence our name *Backstep* for this type of error correction sequence. For example, what would you do if a child left the gross motor area and rather than going directly to the communication area as planned instead walked out of the classroom? Some people might 'redirect' by telling the child where he should go (with possible other prompts). While this fixes the problem- the child ends up in the communication area, we're not sure what the child has learned. Instead, we would correct the error by taking him back in the sequence to the last place he was correct (the gross motor area), re-provide the cue for him to go to the communication area, and then provide the necessary prompts to ensure he gets to that area directly. We teach the correct sequence, rather than fixing incorrect ones. Another example involves teaching a student to wash her hands. She successfully completes the steps in the task analysis up to rinsing but then incorrectly gets a paper towel before turning off the water and leaves the bathroom. Rather than prompting her (with dry hands, standing in the classroom) to turn off the water, we would take her back to the last correctly completed step in the sequence- rinsing hands, have her rinse hands again, then prompt her to turn off the water, and then obtain the paper towel to dry her hands. She must learn to turn the water off before drying her hands, not when we say, "turn off the water." Now her self-care can be praised.

ANTICIPATORY PROMPTS:

For some sequential tasks, Backstepping would be either difficult or impossible. In such cases, we must modify the lesson when it next presents itself. We use *anticipatory prompts* for these sequential lessons. This strategy differs from Backstepping because rather than correcting an error after it has occurred this strategy attempts to prevent errors during the next trial or opportunity. Anticipatory prompts can best be used once the teacher has observed a pattern of errors, and thus can predict when the next error is going to occur. For example, Mary is working on collating 6 papers, stapling them, and placing them in the out-basket. She frequently pauses after placing the stapled bundle in the basket. In general, her teacher must prompt her to start the sequence again. Backstepping wouldn't work because we'd have to take the staple out and that doesn't make sense. Instead, an anticipatory prompt is used by pointing to the first pile of paper when she starts to staple the bundle. Given her history, she is likely to complete stapling and placing the bundle in the basket. However, the point has prompted her to look at the first pile of paper so she is now likely to reach there without pausing after putting the bundle into the basket. To promote independence in the student, the prompt will need to be faded in intensity or moved further and further back in the sequence. That is, instead of providing the prompt when the student is stapling the paper, she is prompted when gathering the pages, then when taking paper #6, then #5, etc. Or, if you are going to fade the intensity of the prompt, then you might initially touch, or even tap the first pile of paper, then just point to it with your finger barely touching it, then pointing to it from 1 foot away, etc.

Guidelines for Completing Data Forms

Andy Bondy and Kate Dickey

This form should be used for completing all lesson plans. Although it appears to require a great deal of information, each area is actually essential to ensure an effective lesson. It is important that all areas of the form are completed, even if 'shorthand' terms are used. Completing all areas of this form will help when problems arise or certain aspects of the lesson are not working as expected (e.g., prompting strategy, error correction, etc.). When a lesson is not effective, we must change something about how the lesson is being taught. Completing and noting later lesson modifications in one location will be helpful over time (and across teachers).

The following guidelines include examples (in italics) for each section of the form.

Student: *Sam*	Teacher: Classroom staff	Date: *1/6/98*

The top of the form starts with the identification of the student and the teacher. The 'teacher' may be one person in particular or consist of a group of people who collaborate on developing and implementing the lesson. The date refers to the date that the lesson plan was developed (or revised).

Behavior objective: Upon encountering a stressful situation, Sam will request a break by approaching a communicative partner and giving a "break" card.
Functional association: Domain: *Communication*   Function: *Escape*

The next area refers to 'behavior objective,' which means defining the target skill. An accurate behavioral objective requires two major components. The first part identifies the conditions under which the behavior will occur (e.g., "Upon encountering a stressful situation"). The second part identifies the specific behavior in measurable terms (e.g., "Sam will request a break by approaching a communicative partner and giving a 'break' card."). The next area of this box refers to 'functional association', which suggests the broad functional relevance of the target skill. For example, the domain for our target skill is noted broadly (e.g., communication), while other possible domains could involve more specific domains, such as 'social' or 'vocational' (implying the specific need to ask for a break in these special situations). Other domains, unrelated to this skill, include: domestic, school-based, community, self-help, and recreation/leisure. Function refers to one of the three primary behavioral functions- 1) gaining access to some type of reinforcer, 2) escape/avoid specific outcomes, or 3) elicited by the situation. The function of the example's skill is identified as escape.

To illustrate the range of options in this area of the form, rather than simply indicating "reading" as the behavior objective within the "school-based" domain, it may be important to note that reading is to be associated with shopping skills, leisure skills (e.g., comic books), or follow a written daily schedule. In this case, the behavior objective could be "reading," occurring under certain condition(s), within the domain "community" and noting that the function of the behavior is to increase independence with shopping skills via reading a shopping list, The point is to describe, in functional terms, where this lesson is heading.

Current lesson status [acquisition, fluency, maintenance]: acquisition
*(*trials/set; # data-points collected per week*): 4 created or spontaneous per day*
Target Criterion (specify type of data: %, frequency, rate, duration, etc.): *80% of opportunities over 3 days*

"Current lesson status" refers to the current extent of the child's ability regarding the skill being taught. If this skill is new to the child, **"acquisition"** should be noted, as in our example. If some aspects of the skill have been acquired but a fair amount of prompting is still needed, then the skill requires refinements in **"fluency."** If the skill has been "mastered" (e.g., rarely requires prompting) but it is still important to make sure that the child is maintaining the skill and/or the skill still needs to be further generalized, then **"maintenance"** would be an appropriate descriptor. This area also provides planning for the number of trials per session or the number of data-points to be taken per week. The "target criterion" should reflect the type of data you will take on this particular behavior. Remember, not all measures involve percent correct. Other measurable aspects of behavior include rate (number per unit time), frequency (number per day), duration (how long the episode lasts), intensity/magnitude (loud vs. soft, hard vs. light, etc.), accuracy (# correct per total number completed), prompt level (moving from physical to gestural prompts), or supervisory level (moving from 1:1 supervision to 4:1 supervision, increasing the distance between supervisor and student, etc.).

Current Stimulus Control: **Needs full physical prompting**	Long-term **cue**: Stressful situations in the classroom

The next area refers to the 'stimulus control' of the particular skill. In general, stimulus control refers to the relationship that certain stimuli come to have over the likelihood that the target (desired) behavior is going to occur. A controlling relationship takes place when a specific stimulus is positively associated with a behavior being reinforced. Such a stimulus is called the discriminative stimulus. Lessons aimed at developing stimulus control should be as functional (natural) as possible. For example, a child may put his shoes on when someone says, "Put on your shoes." However, natural controlling stimuli for putting shoes on would include a) the absence of shoes on feet, b) the presence of reinforcers requiring having on shoes (e.g., going outside to play, entering a store, going into the hallway, etc.). It is also important to remember that a single trial of a stimulus-behavior relationship cannot NOT demonstrate stimulus control (e.g., "give me blue" with only one item on the table) - there must also be an indication of stimuli that do not lead to the desired response (e.g., "give me blue" with several colored items on the table) and stimuli that lead to related behaviors (e.g., "give me red" with several colored items on the table). In other words, to establish a discriminative stimulus you must be sure you can identify at least one stimulus not associated with that behavior.

"Current stimulus control" refers to the stimulus control that now exists for the skill. Examples may include the level of prompt needed for the behavior to occur (e.g., full physical prompt, gesture, model, verbal cue, partial verbal, model, etc.), aspects of the environment (e.g., uses fingers to eat, needs picture to follow instruction, needs chair to sit while working, etc.), aspects of social or supervisory environment (e.g., works if supervisor is within 2 feet, responds only to mom, etc.), or any other potential source of environmental stimulus control. Our example explains that Sam's current control for requesting a break involves "full physical prompting" to exchange the "break" card. "Long-term cue" refers to the stimuli that should come to control this skill once the skill is fully acquired. Examples would involve the same type of stimuli noted earlier (e.g., prompt level, environmental or social cues, etc.). To illustrate, the current stimulus control for a response may involve the student reading a card in the classroom in order to answer the question, "What is your name?" while the long-term cue is to have the student answer this question when asked by a stranger in the community. Our example defines the long-term cue as being "stressful situations in the classroom" which will then trigger Sam to respond, "I need a break." Remember, we eliminate prompts, not cues.

Discrete Trial format: yes (*dispersed trials as needed*) [maximum # per set] one	Sequential format: *no* Chained?: *no*

The next areas deal with the type of lesson being taught. Some lessons involve discrete-trial formats - that is, skills that can be reduced to small, often repeatable steps. If called for, then the teacher should also indicate the maximum number of trials per set. This area is very important to complete so that the teacher avoids running blocks of 10 trials merely because doing so makes calculating the percent correct easier. If all trials are to be conducted during one session, "massed" trials should be noted. If trials are to be dispersed across a large block of time (throughout the school day), then "dispersed" trials should be noted. The number of trials should relate to the skill itself, the level of learning, and characteristics of the student. For example, children 3-years-old and younger should not be made to participate in numerous repeated trials in order to avoid boring the child.

If the lesson involves a number of distinct steps (whether a distinct task-analysis has been written or not) then the "sequential" area should be completed. A task-analysis is written when a skill requires a series of distinct steps. Whether a step is viewed as 'distinct' may merely reflect an opinion. However, if an action is unavoidably part of another action, then it is not distinct. To illustrate, to get a child to throw away a tissue into the garbage can, we would *not* consider 'standing up' a distinct step because it is already part of going to the garbage can. Thus, 'standing up' would not be noted on this task-analysis (though it might be on other activities). It is also important to specify whether the sequence will be taught by way of a backward chain (starting at the end of the sequence) or forward chain (starting from the beginning of the sequence). If there is a task-analysis, the steps should be outlined on the appropriate form. As indicated by our example, teaching will occur for Sam in a discrete trial format (small, repeatable steps) and trials will be dispersed throughout the day. The maximum number of trials per set is one because when Sam is taking a break, the trial cannot be immediately repeated. In addition, we have to wait for Sam to find himself in another stressful situation before we have the opportunity to teach him to exchange the "break" card.

One vs. Two person prompt: **Two**	Prompt Strategy: **Delayed prompting (point/gesture to "break card" and then physical prompting)** Pause interval (for hierarchy or delayed): 1 second progressive time delay (max. 5 seconds)

"One vs. Two person prompt" involves noting whether or not initiation is an important factor for a target communication skill. If initiation is essential, then there must be consideration of whether a two-person prompt strategy will be needed. For example, in the first two phases of PECS, two teachers are used to avoid prompt-dependency. Similarly, when teaching a student to initiate a request for "break" or "help", it should be noted that two teachers would be needed so that the person responding to the request (the communicative partner) is not the one who is also providing the prompts. In our example, we are teaching Sam to request a "break," an issue of initiation, therefore two persons are noted. Following a picture-schedule may require initiation but not two teachers since the picture provides one of the cues. Obviously, not all skills involve child initiation. In general, two-person prompt strategies will involve social or communication objectives.

Also, a description of the "prompt strategy" associated with the lesson is needed. Here, least-to-most prompt hierarchy, most-to-least prompt hierarchy, delayed prompting, modeling, shaping, or fading would be noted. If a strategy requires a pause between prompt levels then note the time interval used. Or if delayed prompting is the strategy, then note either progressive or constant time delay indicating the progression of seconds including the maximum or the second that will remain constant.

Error Correction: Built into procedure (decrease interval next trial)

"Error correction" is documented in the next area. Selecting whether to use a **Backstep, anticipatory prompt**, or the **4-step** should be noted and linked to the type of lesson being taught. If no distinct error correction is needed beyond continuing with the prompt strategy (e.g., graduated guidance, fading, etc.) then make note of that in this space. Given the nature of delayed prompting- a type of errorless learning- errors should not occur. If errors do occur, then noting 'decrease time interval on next trial' is sufficient.

Natural or additional completion R+: *natural: escape*	2nd R+ (during task): praise: "Nice asking for a break"
Current 2nd R+ schedule: *1:1*	Goal 2nd R+ schedule: *1:1*

The next areas deal with the type of 'reinforcement' used for this skill. First, consider the 'natural' consequences for completing this behavior - will it be reinforcing? To illustrate, a natural consequence for putting on sneakers would be to go outside to play. Another example may be setting the table for snack. Many behaviors have identifiable natural reinforcers. However, not all behaviors currently have available natural and/or effective reinforcers. In such cases, 'additional' reinforcers may be needed upon task completion (e.g., tokens, money, free time, access to next activity, etc). In the other box, note the type of secondary or conditioned reinforcers to be used while the task is occurring. For non-repeating discrete trial lessons, this could include giving praise or tokens before the natural consequence is provided. As previously stated, these reinforcers may include labeled-praise, other social reinforcers, immediate tangible reinforcers (e.g., edible, access to a toy, etc.), or they may involve more complex contingencies, such as the use of a 'token system.' In either case, note in the next box the current rate with which this reinforcer is being distributed and then note the long-term goal for this reinforcer schedule. With Sam, the natural reinforcer for requesting a "break" is taking a break from the stressful situation, while his secondary reinforcer includes labeled-praise provided just before his access to the break. His current secondary reinforcer schedule is a one-to-one ratio meaning he gets a break for each request (as well as labeled praise). His goal secondary reinforcer schedule is the same.

Generalization (**stimulus factors**):	Generalization (**response factors**):
[people, place, materials, etc.]	[rate, accuracy, magnitude, duration, supervision, etc.]:
vary staff, activities, materials, locations	student will request a break within 5 seconds of opportunity
	by end of lesson with a supervisor at least 10 feet away

The next areas deal with 'generalization' factors. Remember, do not wait until mastery to consider generalization. The first area considers various types of stimulus factors. These would include different **people, places, materials, activities,** or related factors. Response generalization factors include the **rate** of the behavior per unit time, the **accuracy** of the skill (e.g., number of errors per total work completed), issues associated with the **magnitude** of the response (e.g., loudness, severity, size of work package, etc.), **duration** of the task (e.g., minutes, hours, days, etc.) and **supervisory issues** (e.g., the distance to the supervisor, number of students per supervisor, rate of contact with supervisor per time unit, etc.). With Sam, stimulus factors are defined as his ability to request a break from a variety of staff members, during many different types of activities (circle, work rotations, speech and language therapy, music, etc.), while working with an assortment of different materials (worksheets, arts/crafts, books, vocational materials, etc.) as well as request a break in many different locations. His response factors are defined as per-opportunity and with staff not right next to him.

Parametric details:
Add "break" card to PECS book. Second trainer to be on hand during activities previously identified as troublesome. Breaks to be taken in "break" chair with student prompted to set timer for two minutes prior to sitting down. If student leaves the "break" chair prior to the timer sounding then "break" is over and he must return to activity. Sam should not have access to preferred reinforcers during "break" time.

The section on "parametric details" allows you to note special circumstances associated with the lesson. Issues may include where or when to do the lesson, where the student should physically be relative to the teacher (or other students), special materials needed, etc. Note important factors regarding teaching this lesson rather than writing a finely detailed narrative about all aspects of the lesson.

Data

Trial	Date	Comm. Partner	Prompter	Time delay	Beat the prompt?	Comments
1						
2						
3						
4						
5						

The "data" section permits gathering information about individual trials, or task-analyzed sequences. You may use the key to correspond the types of prompts used (e.g., full physical, partial physical, model, gesture, full verbal, partial verbal, etc.) or add your own keys for various behavior features (e.g., magnitude, duration, etc.). One simple method is to note correct responses ("+") vs. incorrect ("-"). You may also want to note no response ("nr"). The bottom area permits a graphical summation of progress over a relatively short period of time. If this section is NOT completed, then you must note where this information can be found. The above data sheet provides an example of the behaviors that may be tracked with regard to Sam's skill acquisition.

On the following two pages, we share two templates for completing your own lesson plans. The first is the basic template for a discrete lesson with the accompanying data collection grid for customization, the response key and the prompt level key. The second is the basic template for a sequential lesson. It includes a section for writing your task analysis and also includes the response key, prompt level key, and data collection table.

Discrete Lesson Plan Template

Discrete Lesson Plan	Target Skill:

Student:	Teacher:	Date:

Behavior objective:

Functional association: Function:

Current lesson status [acquisition, fluency, maintenance]:
(trials/set; # data-points collected per week):
Target Criterion (specify type of data: %, frequency, rate, duration, etc.):

Current Stimulus Control:	Long-term cue:

Discrete Trial format: [maximum # per set]	Sequential format: Chained?:

One vs. Two person prompt?:	Prompt Strategy: Pause interval (for hierarchy or delayed):

Error Correction:

Natural or additional completion R+:	2nd R+ (during task):
Current 2nd R+ schedule:	Goal 2nd R+ schedule:

Generalization (stimulus factors): [people, place, materials, supervision, etc.]	Generalization (response factors): [rate, accuracy, magnitude, duration, etc.]

Parametric details:

Data Collection

Response Key

Correct: +
Incorrect: -
No response: NR

100										
90										
80										
70										
60										
50										
40										
30										
20										
10										
Date										

Prompt Level Key

FP = full physical
PP = partial physical
M = model
G = gesture
PV = partial verbal
FV = full verbal

Sequential Lesson Plan Template

Sequential Lesson Plan	Target Skill:	

Student:	Teacher:	Date:

Behavior objective:

Functional association: Function:

Current lesson status [acquisition, fluency, maintenance]:
(trials/set; # data-points collected per week):
Target Criterion (specify type of data: %, frequency, rate, duration, etc.):

Current Stimulus Control:	Long-term **cue**:

Discrete Trial format: [maximum # per set]	Sequential format: Chained?:

One vs. Two person prompt?:	Prompt Strategy: Pause interval (for hierarchy or delayed):

Error Correction:

Natural or additional completion R+:	2nd R+ (during task):
Current 2nd R+ schedule:	Goal 2nd R+ schedule:

Generalization (**stimulus factors**): [people, place, materials, supervision, etc.]	Generalization (**response factors**): [rate, accuracy, magnitude, duration, etc.]

Parametric details:

Task Analysis Data Collection

Steps											

Response Key		**Prompt Level Key**
Correct: +	100 / 90 / 80 / 70 / 60 / 50 / 40 / 30 / 20 / 10 / Date	FP = full physical
Incorrect: -		PP = partial physical
No response: NR		M = model
		G = gesture
		PV = partial verbal
		FV = full verbal

Communication Lesson Plans

Discrete Lesson Plan	Target Skill:	Describe multiple objects

Student:	Teacher:	Date:

Behavior objective: Throughout the day, the student will describe objects using two attributes and the object label.
Functional association: Domain: Communication   Function: expressive attributes, descriptive skills, commenting

Current lesson status [acquisition, fluency, maintenance]: acquisition
(trials/set; # data-points collected per week): 2-3 trials/set, 8 data points per week
Target Criterion (specify type of data: %, frequency, rate, duration, etc.): <1 prompt per 5 opportunities, 5 objects, 3 staff

Current **Stimulus Control**: Needs a written prompt	Long-term **cue**: Objects

Discrete Trial format: Yes [maximum # per set] 3 trials/set	Sequential format: No Chained?: No

One vs. Two person prompt?: **One**	**Prompt Strategy**: Fading (written prompt) Pause interval (for hierarchy or delayed):

Error Correction: Use level of assistance needed

Natural or additional completion R+: praise, earns 5 tokens towards trade in	2nd R+ (during task): praise ("Good thinking! That is a big yellow cup!"), tokens
Current 2nd R+ schedule:1:1 praise, tokens	Goal 2nd R+ schedule:1:2 praise, 1:3 tokens

Generalization (**stimulus factors**): [people, place, materials, supervision, etc.] Vary staff, location, activities, and objects	Generalization (**response factors**): [rate, accuracy, magnitude, duration, etc.] Vary number of trials per set, have student describe two objects (e.g., "That's a little green ball and a little blue shovel."), have the student identify objects by description (e.g., "I see something round and blue"), guess what it is.

Parametric details: During activities such as circle time, snack, toy play, or art, show the student an activity related object and a written prompt in the form of (attribute) (attribute) (object). Upon asking the student what the object is, he/she should read the prompt to describe it (e.g., "It's a big, yellow cup"). After three consecutive correct responses, begin to fade the written prompt by making the print lighter in color. Systematically fade the darkness of the print after each three consecutive correct responses. Define each level (e.g., level 1 - regular print, level 2 - one step lighter on the copier, level 5 - lightest available). Indicate objects and attributes, and score + for correct and the level of fading per trial.

Data Collection

Date	Staff	Object	Attribute	Attribute	Level of fading	+/-	Comments

Response Key		**Prompt Level Key**
Correct: + Incorrect: - No response: NR	100 90 80 70 60 50 40 30 20 10 Date	FP = full physical PP = partial physical M = model G = gesture PV = partial verbal FV = full verbal

Discrete Lesson Plan	Target Skill:	**Expressive attributes (with PECS)**

Student:	Teacher:	Date:

Behavior objective: Upon seeing a desired item, the student will request the item including a descriptive attribute.
Functional association: Domain: Communication   Function: requesting specific items

Current lesson status [acquisition, fluency, maintenance]: acquisition
(trials/set; # data-points collected per week): 5 trials/set, 15 data points/week
Target Criterion (specify type of data: %, frequency, rate, duration, etc.): 80% of total opps., across 3 staff, 10 attributes

Current **Stimulus Control**: Holding out 2 items to see which one the students reaches towards	Long-term **cue**: Objects, food, and materials

Discrete Trial format: Yes [maximum # per set]	Sequential format: No Chained? : No

One vs. Two person prompt?: **One**	**Prompt Strategy:** Fading physical prompts Pause interval (for hierarchy or delayed):

Error Correction: Use level of physical assistance needed

Natural or additional completion R+: natural: receives access to requested item, praise	2nd R+ (during task): praise ("Wonderful asking for the <u>red</u> car!")
Current 2nd R+ schedule: 1:1 praise	Goal 2nd R+ schedule: 1:4 praise

Generalization (**stimulus factors**): [people, place, materials, supervision, etc.] Vary staff, materials (e.g., toys, food, arts and crafts), settings (e.g., classroom, kitchen, cafeteria), fade staff proximity	Generalization (**response factors**): [rate, accuracy, magnitude, duration, etc.] Increase number of items to choose from (e.g., color)

Parametric details: Set up opportunities throughout the day within functional activities for the student to make requests using attributes. Initially target highly preferred items that are differentiated by color, size, shape, etc. For example, during an art activity the student requests a button (using PECS) to glue on a shirt. Ask the student, "What color button?" then present the student with a choice of two different colored buttons, after he/she reaches toward one, place that color picture on the front of his/her communication book and full physically prompt him/her to place that picture on his/her sentence strip between the "I want" and the "object" icons. The student will then exchange the sentence strip and be given immediate access. Begin by working on 2 colors. Once the student is 70% accurate, add 2 more colors, etc. Note that if teaching an attribute such as "big" that the polar opposite must also be taught (e.g., "little" in a functional context such as requesting the appropriate size spoon to eat cereal). Contextual cues may be used to aid understanding but working towards eliminating them all together is a goal (e.g. requesting the red ball because it goes in the red hole vs. requesting it because the student wants it).

Data Collection

Date	Staff	Attribute	Object	Prompt level	Comments

Response Key		**Prompt Level Key**
Correct: + Incorrect: - No response: NR	100 90 80 70 60 50 40 30 20 10 Date	FP = full physical PP = partial physical M = model G = gesture PV = partial verbal FV = full verbal

Discrete Lesson Plan	Target Skill:	Expressive body part identification

Student:	Teacher:	Date:

Behavior objective: During activities, such as "Mr. Potato Head" and " Inspector Gadget", the student will request which body part he/she desires in order to participate.
Functional association: Domain: Communication　　Function: body part identification, requesting, participation

Current lesson status [acquisition, fluency, maintenance]: acquisition
(trials/set; # data-points collected per week): 5 trials/set, 12 data points/week
Target Criterion (specify type of data: %, frequency, rate, duration, etc.): 85% of total opportunities, 6 body parts
(head, arm, nose, mouth, eyes, ear)

Current **Stimulus Control**: Needs a gesture to the body part picture	Long-term **cue**: toys, materials, activities

Discrete Trial format: Yes [maximum # per set] 5 trials/set	Sequential format: No Chained?: No

One vs. Two person prompt?: One	**Prompt Strategy**: Delayed Prompting *Pause interval (for hierarchy or delayed):* 1 second progressive time delay (max. 5 sec.)

Error Correction: Built into procedure

Natural or additional completion R+: praise, completing the project/game	2nd R+ (during task): praise ("Excellent asking for the eyes!") 5 tokens earned toward cash out
Current 2nd R+ schedule: 1:1 token, 1:1 praise	Goal 2nd R+ schedule: 1:3 token, 1:3 praise
Generalization (**stimulus factors**): [people, place, materials, supervision, etc.] Vary staff, location, material (e.g., games, art projects), and fade staff proximity	Generalization (**response factors**): [rate, accuracy, magnitude, duration, etc.] Increase the number of body parts in array

Parametric details: During structured activities such as "Mr. Potato Head" and "Inspector Gadget" have the student request which body part he/she would like using PECS. For example, "I want eyes." Begin by holding out one body part in your hand. As the student puts together his/her sentence strip, point/gesture to the corresponding picture of the item that you are holding. Begin by introducing 2 body parts. Once the student is 70% accurate, add 2 more body parts. Begin with zero time delay and continue to increase the time delay by one-second increments after every 5 correct trials. Record "+" if the student beats the prompt and a "-" if the student does not beat the prompt.

Data Collection

Date	Staff	Activity	Body part	Time delay	Beat the prompt?	Comments

Response Key		**Prompt Level Key**
Correct: + Incorrect: - No response: NR	100 / 90 / 80 / 70 / 60 / 50 / 40 / 30 / 20 / 10 / Date	FP = full physical PP = partial physical M = model G = gesture PV = partial verbal FV = full verbal

Sequential Lesson Plan	Target Skill:	Follow object schedule

Student:	Teacher:	Date:

Behavior objective: To move from one activity to the next, the student will follow an object schedule.

Functional association: Domain: Communication   Function: organization of day, increase independence

Current lesson status [acquisition, fluency, maintenance]: acquisition
(trials/set; # data-points collected per week): 5 data points per week
Target Criterion (specify type of data: %, frequency, rate, duration, etc.): 80% accuracy across 3 staff

Current **Stimulus Control**: Needs full physical prompting	Long-term **cue**: Activity finished

Discrete Trial format: No [maximum # per set]	Sequential format: Yes Chained?: Backward Chain

One vs. Two person prompt?: **One**	**Prompt Strategy**: Fading - FP, PP, G Pause interval (for hierarchy or delayed):

Error Correction: Backstep (then decrease independent distance on next trial)

Natural or additional completion R+: praise, access to next activity, token at completion of task	2nd R+ (during task): praise ("Great getting your work materials!") token at completion of task
Current 2nd R+ schedule: praise at completion of target step	Goal 2nd R+ schedule: praise at end of task

Generalization (**stimulus factors**): [people, place, materials, supervision, etc.] Vary trainers, materials, location of materials	Generalization (**response factors**): [rate, accuracy, magnitude, duration, etc.] Fade staff proximity, increase number of tasks

Parametric details: Student must be able to follow directions with individual object symbols. Materials to be obtained must be functionally relevant. Set up the student's object schedule prior to his/her arrival each day. Each symbol must have a corresponding green square where the corresponding materials are located. Fully prompt the student through all of the steps of the task analysis until the last step. Teach this by fading physical and gestural prompts. Indicate the level of prompt needed. Once a criterion is met on the last step add the prior step to the sequence. Allow the student to independently complete remaining step(s). There should be NO verbal prompts given during this lesson. Initially, all prompts should be physical and then gestural.

Task Analysis Data Collection

Steps Date:										
1. Upon completion of activity, returns materials										
2. Takes symbol off of green card										
3. Takes to schedule and puts in finished box										
4. Takes next symbol off of schedule										
5. Takes symbol to area where materials are found										
6. Places symbol on appropriate green card										
7. Gets appropriate materials										
8. Takes materials to work area										
Total:										
Staff:										

Response Key Correct: + Incorrect: - No response: NR	100 90 80 70 60 50 40 30 20 10 Date											**Prompt Level Key** FP = full physical PP = partial physical M = model G = gesture PV = partial verbal FV = full verbal

Discrete Lesson Plan	Target Skill:	Follow one step spoken directions: Version 1

Student:	Teacher:	Date:

Behavior objective: Throughout the day, the student will follow one step verbal directions.
Functional association: Domain: School Based   Function: receptive language, direction following

Current lesson status [acquisition, fluency, maintenance]: acquisition
(trials/set; # data-points collected per week):1 trials/set, 5 data points per week
Target Criterion (specify type of data: %, frequency, rate, duration, etc.): 80% accuracy, 5 directions, 3 staff

Current **Stimulus Control**: Needs full physical prompting	Long-term **cue**: A verbal direction

Discrete Trial format: Yes [maximum # per set] 1 trial/set	Sequential format: No Chained?: No

One vs. Two person prompt? **One**	**Prompt Strategy**: Most to Least Prompt Hierarchy - FP, PP, G Pause interval (for hierarchy or delayed):

Error Correction: Provide sufficient prompt level

Natural or additional completion R+: natural: continues with current activity, praise, token	2nd R+ (during task): praise ("Great putting the bottle in the refrigerator."), token
Current 2nd R+ schedule: 1:1 praise, 1:1 token	Goal 2nd R+ schedule: 1:2 praise, 1:2 token for independent responses

Generalization (**stimulus factors**): [people, place, materials, supervision, etc.] Vary directions, staff, activities (e.g., cooking, art, gym), locations, fade staff proximity	Generalization (**response factors**): [rate, accuracy, magnitude, duration etc.] Increase distance to items

Parametric details: Work on this skill within other activities such as cooking, gym, circle, trips, and art. Give the student the direction (e.g. while cooking: "Put the bottle in the refrigerator.", "Get a bowl.", "Stir.", while in art: "Get the scissors.", Get the ____ paint.", etc.) and fully prompt him/her to complete the direction. Fade the intensity of prompting to partial physical and then to a gesture as the student becomes more independent with the task direction. Indicate the level of prompt given or "+" if completed independently. Be sure to mix up activities, directions, materials, items, and settings so you can be sure that the student is following the direction given and not just responding because they know what to do with a particular object, heard a key word, or has learned what to do in a particular setting or situation, etc.

Data Collection

Date	Staff	Activity	Direction given	Prompt level	Comments

Response Key	100												**Prompt Level Key**
	90												
	80												
Correct: +	70												FP = full physical
	60												PP = partial physical
Incorrect: -	50												
No response: NR	40												M = model
	30												G = gesture
	20												PV = partial verbal
	10												
	Date												FV = full verbal

Discrete Lesson Plan	Target Skill:	Follow one step spoken directions: Version 2

Student:	Teacher:	Date:

Behavior objective: Throughout the school day, the student will follow one step spoken directions.
Functional association: Domain: Communication   Function: direction following, independent living

Current lesson status [acquisition, fluency, maintenance]: fluency
(trials/set; # data-points collected per week): 1 trial/set, 2 data points per week (for each direction being taught)
Target Criterion (specify type of data: %, frequency, rate, duration, etc.): 80% accuracy across 3 staff, 3 settings

Current **Stimulus Control**: Directions given within the classroom requires partial prompting	Long-term **cue** : Spoken directions

Discrete Trial format: Yes [maximum # per set] 1 trial/opportunity	Sequential format : No Chained? : No

One vs. Two person prompt?: **One**	**Prompt Strategy**: Fading - FP,PP, G Pause interval (for hierarchy or delayed):

Error Correction: Backstep (then decrease independent distance on next trial)

Natural or additional completion R+ : natural access to next activity: "line up" = playground, praise	2nd R+ (during task): praise ("Good job throwing that away.")
Current 2nd R+ schedule: 1:1	Goal 2nd R+ schedule:1:4

Generalization (**stimulus factors**): [people, place, materials, supervision, etc.] Vary activities, staff, materials, settings (e.g., classroom, hallways, cafeteria, community sites), and staff proximity	Generalization (**response factors**): [rate, accuracy, magnitude, duration, etc.]

Parametric details: Throughout the school day have the student follow functional directions. To begin, give the direction and immediately fully prompt student through action. After 5 trials of fully prompting him/her (to the item), stop one foot away from (the item) and let him/her finish the last step. Once the student has 4 successful trials in a row, then stop 2 feet from (the item) and let him/her finish the direction independently. Continue this fading procedure until the student is following the direction independently. Make sure the directions given are incorporated into functional activities and materials to be obtained are functionally relevant. Avoid mass trial format (unless it fits the functional activity). Some examples include: line up, come here, throw away, give to (involves actions), put in book bag (involves action with object) and get (involves object selection). Initially, training should involve the same 'type' of direction. Once learned, then they can be interspersed.

Data Collection

Date	Staff							Comments

Response Key		**Prompt Level Key**
Correct: + Incorrect: - No response: NR	100 / 90 / 80 / 70 / 60 / 50 / 40 / 30 / 20 / 10 / Date	FP = full physical PP = partial physical M = model G = gesture PV = partial verbal FV = full verbal

Pyramid Educational Consultants

Sequential Lesson Plan	Target Skill:	Follow a picture schedule

Student:	Teacher:	Date:

Behavior objective: To transition from one activity to another, the student will follow a picture schedule.

Functional association: Domain: Communication   Function: transitions, move independently through day

Current lesson status [acquisition, fluency, maintenance]: acquisition
(trials/set; # data-points collected per week): 1 trial/set, 5 data points per week
Target Criterion (specify type of data: %, frequency, rate, duration, etc.): < 1 prompt/trial per 5 opportunities

Current **Stimulus Control**: Fully prompted to move pictures on schedule	Long-term **cue**: Activity finished

Discrete Trial format: No [maximum # per set]	Sequential format: Yes Chained?: Backward Chain

One vs. Two person prompt?: **One**	**Prompt Strategy**: Fading - FP, PP, G, Pause interval (for hierarchy or delayed):

Error Correction: Backstep (then decrease independent distance on next trial)

Natural or additional completion R+: praise, access to next activity, token	2nd R+ (during task): praise ("Great putting the picture in the finished envelope.")
Current 2nd R+ schedule: 1:1 completion of changing schedule	Goal 2nd R+ schedule: change schedule and move to next activity independently (fade token)

Generalization (**stimulus factors**): [people, place, materials supervision, etc.] Vary staff, activities, materials (e.g., schedule for tooth brushing routine), and place (e.g., bathroom, kitchen), fade staff proximity	Generalization (**response factors**): [rate, accuracy, magnitude, duration, etc.] Increase number of tasks

Parametric details: Student must be able to follow directions with individual picture symbols. Materials to be obtained must be functionally relevant. Begin by fully prompting the student from the last activity to the schedule board. Fully prompt him/her through the entire task until the last step. Teach this by fading physical and gestural prompts. After 3 correct responses on the target step, add the second to last step to the sequence. Allow the student to complete the remaining step(s) independently. There should be NO verbal prompts given during this lesson. Initially, all prompts should be physical and then gestural.

Task Analysis Data Collection

Steps Date:											
1. Student goes to schedule after completion of activity											
2. Removes picture off the top of the schedule/or "Working on" card											
3. Places it in the finished pocket											
4. Removes next picture on the schedule											
5. Places it at the top of the schedule board/or on "Working on" card											
6. Goes to the next activity											
Total:											
Staff:											

Response Key

Correct: +
Incorrect: -
No response: NR

100											
90											
80											
70											
60											
50											
40											
30											
20											
10											
Date											

Prompt Level Key

FP = full physical
PP = partial physical
M = model
G = gesture
PV = partial verbal
FV = full verbal

Sequential Lesson Plan	Target Skill:	Following a direction given a picture

Student:	Teacher:	Date:

Behavior objective: When given a picture and a verbal direction, "Get this", the student will get the item.

Functional association: Domain: Communication   Function: direction following

Current lesson status [acquisition, fluency, maintenance]: acquisition
(trials/set; # data-points collected per week): 7 trials/set, 8 data points per week
Target Criterion (specify type of data: %, frequency, rate, duration, etc.): 85%/10 pictures, across 3 staff

Current **Stimulus Control**: Needs full physical prompting	Long-term **cue**: Picture on daily schedule

Discrete Trial format: No *[maximum # per set]* 7/set (dispersed throughout day)	Sequential format: Yes Chained?: No

One vs. Two person prompt?: **One**	**Prompt Strategy**: Fading physical prompts - FP, PP, G Pause interval (for hierarchy or delayed:

Error Correction: Backstep (then decrease independent distance on next trial)

Natural or additional completion R+: natural: getting needed item (e.g., spoon for cereal), praise	2nd R+ (during task): praise ("Nice getting the spoon.")
Current 2nd R+ schedule: 1:1 praise	Goal 2nd R+ schedule: 1:4 praise

Generalization (**stimulus factors**): [people, place, materials, supervision, etc.] Vary staff, location (e.g., kitchen, group home, home), pictures of items (e.g., spoon, puzzle), fade staff proximity	Generalization (**response factors**): [rate, accuracy, magnitude, duration, etc.] Fade picture as appropriate, increase # items retrieved

Parametric details: Materials used must be familiar to student (e.g., there is an established functional use for each object). Hand the student the picture and give the direction, "Get this." Then fully prompt the student to the item. After 5 trials of fully prompting him/her to the item, stop one foot away from the item and let him/her finish the last step. Once the student has 4 successful trials in a row, then stop 2 feet from the item and let him/her finish the direction independently. Continue to systematically increase the distance between the student and the retrievable item.

Data Collection

Date	Staff	Prompt	1 foot	2 feet	3 feet	4 feet	5 feet	7 feet	9 feet	Comments

Response Key		**Prompt Level Key**

Response Key

Correct: +
Incorrect: -
No response: NR

| 100 |
| 90 |
| 80 |
| 70 |
| 60 |
| 50 |
| 40 |
| 30 |
| 20 |
| 10 |
| Date |

Prompt Level Key

FP = full physical
PP = partial physical
M = model
G = gesture
PV = partial verbal
FV = full verbal

Pyramid Educational Consultants

Discrete Lesson Plan	Target Skill:	Gaining eye contact (PECS)

Student:	Teacher:	Date:

Behavior objective: When needing a communicative partner's attention, the student will approach, gain eye-contact, and then deliver his/her message.
Functional association: Domain: Communication   Function: gain attention appropriately, gain eye-contact, social skills

Current lesson status [acquisition, fluency, maintenance]: acquisition
(trials/set; # data-points collected per week): 4 created or spontaneous per day
Target Criterion (specify type of data: %, frequency, rate, duration, etc.): 85 % of total opportunities across 3 staff

Current **Stimulus Control** :Needs full physical prompts	Long-term **cue**: Communicative partner and message

Discrete Trial format: Yes [maximum # per set] 1 trial/set	Sequential format: No Chained?: No

One vs. Two person prompt?: **Requires One to physically prompt and One to respond**	**Prompt Strategy**: Delayed Prompting *Pause interval (for hierarchy or delayed):* 1 second progressive time delay (max. 5 secs.)

Error Correction: Built into procedure

Natural or additional completion R+: natural: receives attention, immediate 1:1, praise	2nd R+ (during task): praise ("Good getting my attention.")
Current 2nd R+ schedule: 1:1 praise	Goal 2nd R+ schedule: 1:1 natural: receives attention only

Generalization (**stimulus factors**): [people, place, materials, supervision, etc.] Vary staff, location, materials and activities, have communication partner move farther away	Generalization (**response factors**): [rate, accuracy, magnitude, duration, etc.] Generalize to different requests (e.g., need bathroom), say "Excuse me" to gain attention

Parametric details: Create an opportunity for the student to request materials, reinforcers, and/or help. Begin teaching with a time delay of zero by immediately (after the student has a completed sentence strip in hand) fully physically prompting the student to the communicative partner, fully prompting the student to gain eye-contact by placing his/her hand on the communicative partner's face and gently moving the communicative partner's face toward his/her own until eye-contact has been established. Gradually increase the time delay by one second increments until the student is beating the prompt.

Data Collection

Date	Trainer	Communicative partner	Time delay	Beat the prompt?	Proximity to comm. partner	Comments

Response Key		**Prompt Level Key**
Correct: + Incorrect: - No response: NR	100 90 80 70 60 50 40 30 20 10 Date	FP = full physical PP = partial physical M = model G = gesture PV = partial verbal FV = full verbal

Discrete Lesson Plan		Target Skill:	Gaining staff attention

Student:	Teacher:	Date:

Behavior objective: When needing staff attention, the student will approach an adult and tap them on the upper arm.
Functional association: Domain: Communication   Function: gaining attention appropriately, social skills

Current lesson status [acquisition, fluency, maintenance]: acquisition
(trials/set; # data-points collected per week) 3 created or spontaneous per day
Target Criterion (specify type of data: %, frequency, rate, duration, etc.): 85% of total opportunities across 3 staff

Current **Stimulus Control**: Needs a model from staff	Long-term **cue**: Objects, materials, or help

Discrete Trial format: Yes [maximum # per set] 1 trial/set	Sequential format: No Chained?: No

One vs. Two person prompt?: **Requires one to model and one to respond**	**Prompt Strategy**: Delayed Prompting (model tapping communicative partner's arm)
	Pause interval (for hierarchy or delayed): 1 second progressive time delay

Error Correction: Built into procedure

Natural or additional completion R+: natural: receives attention, immediate 1:1, praise	2nd R+ (during task): praise ("Good getting my attention.")
Current 2nd R+ schedule: 1:1 praise	Goal 2nd R+ schedule: 1:1 natural: receives attention only

Generalization (**stimulus factors**): [people, place, materials, supervision, etc.] Vary staff, location, materials and activities, have communicative partner move farther away	Generalization (**response factors**): [rate, accuracy, magnitude, duration, etc.] Generalize to different requests (e.g., need bathroom), say "Excuse me" to gain attention

Parametric details: The student must be able to respond to a model gaining attention. Create an opportunity for the student to request materials, reinforcers, and/or help. Begin teaching with a time delay of zero by immediately modeling gaining the communicative partner's attention by approaching and tapping the upper arm. Gradually increase the time delay by one second increments until the student is successfully beating the prompt and criteria is met.

Data Collection

Date	Trainer	Communicative partner	Length of time delay	Beat the prompt?	Proximity to communicative partner	Comments

Response Key

Correct: +
Incorrect: -
No response: NR

100											
90											
80											
70											
60											
50											
40											
30											
20											
10											
Date											

Prompt Level Key

FP = full physical
PP = partial physical
M = model
G = gesture
PV = partial verbal
FV = full verbal

Discrete Lesson Plan	Target Skill:	Indicating "finished"

Student:	Teacher:	Date:

Behavior objective: When the student has completed an activity, he/she will let a staff member know by exchanging a "finished" picture or by saying "finished"/"I'm finished".

Functional association: Domain: Communication   Function: communication skills, independent work skills

Current lesson status [acquisition, fluency, maintenance]: acquisition
(trials/set; # data-points collected per week): 1 trial/set, 3 data points per week
Target Criterion (specify type of data: %, frequency, rate, duration, etc.): <1 prompt/5 trials, 3 staff, 4 activities

Current **Stimulus Control**: Needs full physical prompting	Long-term **cue**: Work completed

Discrete Trial format: Yes [maximum # per set] 1 trial/set	Sequential format: No Chained?: No

One vs. Two person prompt?: **Two**	**Prompt Strategy**: Fading - FP, PP, M, G Pause interval (for hierarchy or delayed):

Error Correction:

Natural or additional completion R+: praise, access to next activity, edible	2nd R+ (during task): n/a
Current 2nd R+ schedule: 1:1 praise, 1:1 small edible	Goal 2nd R+ schedule: 1:3 praise

Generalization (**stimulus factors**): [people, place, materials, supervision, etc.] Vary staff, activities being completed (e.g., folding laundry, legos, sorting utensils), work locations, fade trainer	Generalization (**response factors**): [rate, accuracy, magnitude, duration, etc.] Fade staff proximity once the student is more independent with the task so that he/she must approach a staff member to tell them he/she is finished

Parametric details: Work on this skill with activities that have a clearly defined endpoint (e.g., using up all the legos in a bowl, folding all the towels in a basket). Initially, when the student completes an activity the communicative partner should approach him/her while the trainer prompts the student to indicate "finished" using one of the above mentioned forms. The communicative partner should provide the praise and reinforcement. Fade the trainer prompts and then the trainer as appropriate. Eventually fade the proximity of the communicative partner so that the student learns to approach him/her to indicate that he/she is finished with the activity/work.

Data Collection

Date	Trainer	Communicative partner	Proximity of communicative partner	Prompt level	Completed activity/work	Comments

Response Key	**Prompt Level Key**
Correct: + Incorrect: - No response: NR	FP = full physical PP = partial physical M = model G = gesture PV = partial verbal FV = full verbal

100
90
80
70
60
50
40
30
20
10
Date

Discrete Lesson Plan	Target Skill:	Personal information

Student:	Teacher:	Date:

Behavior objective: During activities, such as "Lotto" and "Twister", the student will answer personal information questions.

Functional association: Domain: Communication   Function: independent living skills, social skills, communication

Current lesson status [acquisition, fluency, maintenance]: acquisition
(trials/set; # data-points collected per week): 4 trials/set (4 answers on game board), 12 data points/week
Target Criterion (specify type of data: %, frequency, rate, duration, etc.): 4/5 opportunities w/o prompting , 4 concepts
(name, address, phone number, age)

Current **Stimulus Control**: Needs matching colors for question and answer	Long-term **cue**: Questions

Discrete Trial format: Yes [maximum # per set] 4	Sequential format: No Chained?: No

One vs. Two person prompt?: **One**	**Prompt Strategy**: Fading (colored written prompt) Pause interval (for hierarchy or delayed):

Error Correction: Use level of color needed (fade color of question and answer one step closer to black each time the student answers question correctly 3 consecutive times) Darken cue following error

Natural or additional completion R+: praise, continuation of game	2nd R+ (during task): praise ("You're right! You are 5 years old!") 5 tokens earned toward cash out
Current 2nd R+ schedule: 1:1 token, 1:1 praise	Goal 2nd R+ schedule: 1:2 token 1:1 praise

Generalization (**stimulus factors**): [people, place, materials, supervision, etc.] Vary staff, locations, games played, location of answers on game board, have other students ask the questions, introduce questions after the game	Generalization (**response factors**): [rate, accuracy, magnitude, duration, etc.] Increase number of answers on board, increase number of times you play the game

Parametric details: During structured activities such as "Lotto" and "Twister", using a modified game board, have the student answer personal information questions. To modify game boards, put personal information such as name, age, address, and phone number in the boxes. To begin, color code questions to the correct answers. Staff will show and read cards with colored questions to the student. Some questions may be: "How old are you?" and "Where do you live?" The student will locate the appropriate answer on his/her game board. Gradually fade color of questions and answers to black as student becomes more independent with responding. Indicate level of fading per question/answer (e.g., level 2 out of 6).

Data Collection

Date	Staff	Game	Name	Age	Address	Phone number	Comments	

Response Key

Correct: +
Incorrect: -
No response: NR

100										
90										
80										
70										
60										
50										
40										
30										
20										
10										
Date										

Prompt Level Key

FP = full physical
PP = partial physical
M = model
G = gesture
PV = partial verbal
FV = full verbal

Pyramid Educational Consultants

Discrete Lesson Plan	Target Skill:	Relaying information about an errand

Student:	Teacher:	Date:

Behavior objective: After running an errand (e.g. delivering a message, retrieving an object), the student will answer questions about the errand.

Functional association: Domain: Communication   Function: social skills, factual recall skills

Current lesson status [acquisition, fluency, maintenance]: acquisition
(trials/set; # data-points collected per week): 1 trial/set, 3 data points per week
Target Criterion (specify type of data: %, frequency, rate, duration, etc.): <1 prompt/5 trials, 3 staff, 3 questions

Current **Stimulus Control**: Needs a model	Long-term **cue**: Question(s) regarding errands
Discrete Trial format: Yes [maximum # per set] 1 trial/set	Sequential format: No Chained?: No

One vs. Two person prompt?: **One**	**Prompt Strategy**: Delayed Prompting *Pause interval (for hierarchy or delayed):* 1 second progressive time delay (max.5 secs.)

Error Correction: Built into procedure (decrease interval on next trial)

Natural or additional completion R+: praise, small edible, access to next activity	2nd R+ (during task): praise ("Great job telling me who you saw.")
Current 2nd R+ schedule: 1:1 praise, 1:1 small edible	Goal 2nd R+ schedule: 1:5 praise, fade out edible

Generalization (**stimulus factors**): [people, place, materials, supervision, etc.] Vary staff, people interacted with on errands, location of errands, types of errands (e.g., delivering messages and objects, retrieving objects), and questions asked.	Generalization (**response factors**): [rate, accuracy, magnitude, duration, etc.] Increase number of questions asked about an errand, increase time between errand and question

Parametric details: Following an errand ask, "What did you get?" Then teach, "Where did you go?" and "Who did you see?" Begin using zero time delay: after the student returns from running the errand, ask the target question and then immediately model the correct response ("I got ____."). Increase the time delay by one-second increments (e.g., 2 sec. time delay, then 3 sec. time delay, 4 sec. and 5 sec.) until the student is reliably beating the prompt. Record "+" if the student beats the prompt and "-" if the student does not beat the prompt. When the student requires <2 prompts/5 trials for "What did you get?" begin teaching "Where did you go?" When the student requires <2 prompts/5 trials for these two questions, begin teaching "Who did you see?" Make sure to "plan" rotating the questions asked so that you are sure to intersperse them. This is important for generalization purposes, and to ensure learned responses not just rote responses.

Data Collection

Date	Staff	Length of time delay	Beat the prompt?	Question asked	Response	Comments

Response Key		**Prompt Level Key**
Correct: + Incorrect: - No response: NR	100 90 80 70 60 50 40 30 20 10 Date	FP = full physical PP = partial physical M = model G = gesture PV = partial verbal FV = full verbal

Discrete Lesson Plan	Target Skill:	Requesting a break

Student:	Teacher:	Date:

Behavior objective: During undesirable activities or situations, the student will request a break when needed.
Functional association: Domain: Communication   Function: social skills, communication, decreases frustration

Current lesson status [acquisition, fluency, maintenance]: acquisition
(trials/set; # data-points collected per week): 1 trial per set, 5 data points per week
Target Criterion (specify type of data: %, frequency, rate, duration, etc.): <1 prompt/5 trials, 2 staff

Current **Stimulus Control**: Needs full physical prompting	Long-term **cue**: An activity or situation and a "break" symbol

Discrete Trial format: Yes [maximum # per set] 1 trial per set	Sequential format: No Chained?: No

One vs. Two person prompt?: **Two**	**Prompt Strategy**: Fading - FP, PP, G Pause interval (for hierarchy or delayed):

Error Correction: Use prompt level needed

Natural or additional completion R+: natural: escapes the situation temporarily, praise	2nd R+ (during task): praise ("Great asking for a break.")
Current 2nd R+ schedule: 1:1 praise	Goal 2nd R+ schedule: 1:5 praise
Generalization (**stimulus factors**): [people, place, materials supervision, etc.] Vary staff, locations, activities (e.g., group game, visual model activity, cleaning), fade staff proximity	Generalization (**response factors**): [rate, accuracy, magnitude, duration, etc.] Decrease the length of the break, reduce number of breaks per activity

Parametric details: Initially, use two staff to teach this skill. Upon the occurrence of agitating or frustrating circumstances (e.g., high rate of demand, long task, hard task), the prompter should fully physically prompt the student to hand the communicative partner a break card. The communicative partner should immediately respond, "Go ahead, take a break." The break should occur in a designated area for no longer than two minutes. Use a timer to signal that break is finished (teach the child to set the timer upon entering the break area). If the student leaves the designated area before the timer sounds then break is over. The student should not have access to preferred activities or reinforcers while on break but may have low-level reinforcers. When break is over, remind student of next available reinforcer(s). As the student becomes more independent with requesting a break, the prompter should fade use of physical assistance. Eventually, fading out the prompter altogether.

Data Collection

Date	Staff	Activity	Communicative partner	Prompter	Prompt level	# of breaks/ activity	Comments

Response Key		**Prompt Level Key**
Correct: + Incorrect: - No response: NR	100 / 90 / 80 / 70 / 60 / 50 / 40 / 30 / 20 / 10 / Date	FP = full physical PP = partial physical M = model G = gesture PV = partial verbal FV = full verbal

Discrete Lesson Plan	Target Skill:	Requesting help (card)

Student:	Teacher:	Date:

Behavior objective: When the student cannot open an item or needs help with an activity, he/she will exchange a visual symbol of "help" to a communicative partner.
Functional association: Domain: Communication   Function: requesting help, decrease frustration level

Current lesson status [acquisition, fluency, maintenance]: acquisition
(trials/set; # data-points collected per week): 5 created or spontaneous per day, 5 data points per week
Target Criterion (specify type of data: %, frequency, rate, duration, etc.): 80% accuracy across 3 staff

Current **Stimulus Control**: Needs full physical prompting	Long-term cue: Problem situation and help symbol

Discrete Trial format: Yes [maximum # per set] 4 trials/day	Sequential format: No Chained? No

One vs. Two person prompt?: **Two**	**Prompt Strategy**: Fading - FP, PP, G Pause interval (for hierarchy or delayed):

Error Correction: Provide prompt level needed

Natural or additional completion R+: natural: receives help	2nd R+ (during task): praise ("Nice asking for help.")
Current 2nd R+ schedule: 1:1 praise	Goal 2nd R+ schedule: 1:4 praise

Generalization (**stimulus factors**): [people, place, materials, supervision, etc.] Vary trainers, items (e.g., containers with preferred foods or toys inside, juice box w/straw attached, a toy which requires a button to push to turn it on), location, and fade staff proximity	Generalization (**response factors**): [rate, accuracy, magnitude, duration, etc.]

Parametric details: Begin by setting up a situation in which the student will need help. BEFORE the student gets frustrated with the item/activity he/she needs help with, the physical prompter (person behind the student) will fully physically prompt the student to exchange the visual symbol of "help" (or helping hand icon) to the communicative partner. Because this is a new lesson, have only the help symbol in front of the student either on their communication book or on the desk. The physical prompter should begin to fade proximity and assistance as the student becomes more independent. Once the student begins to have success, the physical prompter should remain in the area if their assistance should be needed.

Data Collection

Date	Prompter	Communication partner	Item/activity/ type of help	Visual symbol exchange	Comments

Response Key	100											**Prompt Level Key**
	90										
	80										
Correct: +	70										FP = full physical
Incorrect: -	60										PP = partial physical
	50										
No response: NR	40										M = model
	30										G = gesture
	20										PV = partial verbal
	10										FV = full verbal
	Date										

Discrete Lesson Plan	Target Skill:	Requesting help (with item)

Student:	Teacher:	Date

Behavior objective: When the student needs help opening an item, he/she will bring that item to staff.

Functional association: Domain: Communication   Function: requesting help, decrease frustration level

Current lesson status [acquisition, fluency, maintenance]: acquisition
(trials/set; # data-points collected per week): 5 created or spontaneous per day, 5 data points per week
Target Criterion (specify type of data: %, frequency, rate, duration, etc.): 80% accuracy across 3 staff

Current **Stimulus Control**: Needs full physical prompting	Long-term **cue**: Unopened item

Discrete Trial format: Yes [maximum # per set] 5 trials/day	Sequential format: No Chained? No

One vs. Two person prompt?: **Two**	**Prompt Strategy**: Fading - FP, PP, G Pause interval (for hierarchy or delayed);

Error Correction: Provide prompt level needed

Natural or additional completion R+: natural: receives help	2nd R+ (during task): praise ("Nice asking for help.")
Current 2nd R+ schedule: 1:1 praise	Goal 2nd R+ schedule: 1:4 praise

Generalization (**stimulus factors**): [people, place, materials, supervision, etc.] Vary trainers, items (e.g., containers with preferred foods or toys inside, juice box w/ straw attached, a toy which requires a button be pushed to turn it on), location, and fade staff proximity	Generalization (**response factors**): [rate, accuracy, magnitude, duration, etc.]

Parametric details: Set up a situation where the student will have difficulty opening an item. BEFORE the student gets frustrated, the physical prompter should fully prompt the student to pick up the item, approach and hand it to the communicative partner. The partner immediately provides help and praise. As the student begins to have success, the physical prompter should fade prompting level and proximity. Once the student is able to independently hand the item to the communicative partner, then he/she can begin to exchange a visual symbol of "help." See lesson called "Request help (card)."

Data Collection

Date	Trainer	Communicative partner	Item	Prompt	Comments

Response Key

Correct: +
Incorrect: -
No response: NR

100											
90											
80											
70											
60											
50											
40											
30											
20											
10											
Date											

Prompt Level Key

FP = full physical
PP = partial physical
M = model
G = gesture
PV = partial verbal
FV = full verbal

Pyramid Educational Consultants

Discrete Lesson Plan	Target Skill:	Requesting specific help (spoken)

Student:	Teacher:	Date:

Behavior objective: When encountering an obstacle, the student will request specific help by saying, "I need help with _____."

Functional association: Domain: Communication   Function: increase independence/decrease frustration

Current lesson status [acquisition, fluency, maintenance]: fluency
(trials/set; # data-points collected per week): 3 created or spontaneous per day
Target Criterion (specify type of data: %, frequency, rate, duration, etc.): 80% of total opportunities across 3 staff

Current **Stimulus Control**: Needs a model from staff	Long-term **cue**: Obstacle

Discrete Trial format: Yes [maximum # per set] 1 trial/set	Sequential format: No Chained?: No

One vs. Two person prompt?: **One**	**Prompt Strategy**: Delayed Prompting (model "I need help with _____.") Pause interval (for hierarchy or delayed): 1 second progressive time delay

Error Correction: Built into procedure

Natural or additional completion R+: natural: receives help, immediate 1:1, praise	2nd R+ (during task): praise ("Very nice asking for help.")
Current 2nd R+ schedule: 1:1 praise	Goal 2nd R+ schedule: 1:1 natural: receives help only

Generalization (**stimulus factors**): [people, place, materials, supervision, etc.] Vary staff, location, materials and activities (e.g., tight lids on jars, starting computer games, following a model during art) , and fade communicative partner proximity	Generalization (**response factors**): [rate, accuracy, magnitude, duration, etc.] Generalize to specifying the action for which the student needs help, for example, "I want help open door".

Parametric details: Begin by setting up a situation in which the student will need help. When the student requests help (non-specifically) immediately model the specific request for help, "I need help with ____." Provide help following imitation of the specific request. Increase the time delay to one second when the student successfully imitates the model for three consecutive trials. Continue to increase the time delay by one-second increments (e.g., 2 sec. time delay, then 3 sec., 4 sec., etc.) as the student appropriately imitates requests for specific help. The goal is for the student to beat the prompt.

Data Collection

Date	Trainer	Length of time delay	Beat the prompt?	Situation	Proximity to communicative partner	Comments

Response Key		**Prompt Level Key**
Correct: + Incorrect: - No response: NR	100 90 80 70 60 50 40 30 20 10 Date	FP = full physical PP = partial physical M = model G = gesture PV = partial verbal FV = full verbal

Discrete Lesson Plan	Target Skill:	Responding gesturally yes/no (to an offer)

Student:	Teacher:	Date:

Behavior objective: When presented with an item and asked, "Do you want _____?" the student will use the appropriate head gesture to respond yes or no.
Functional association: Domain: Communication   Function: communication skills, independent living skills

Current lesson status [acquisition, fluency, maintenance]: acquisition
(trials/set; # data-points collected per week): 1-5 trials/set, 5 data points per week
Target Criterion (specify type of data: %, frequency, rate, duration, etc.): 80% accuracy, 3 staff, 5 items

Current **Stimulus Control**: Needs full physical prompting	Long-term **cue**: Question

Discrete Trial format: Yes [maximum # per set] 5 trials/set	Sequential format: No Chained?: No

One vs. Two person prompt?: **Two**	**Prompt Strategy**: Fading - FP, PP, M Pause interval (for hierarchy or delayed):

Error Correction: Use appropriate level of prompt

Natural or additional completion R+: natural: gets access to item/does not get access to item, praise	2nd R+ (during task): praise ("Great shaking your head yes!")
Current 2nd R+ schedule: 1:1 praise	Goal 2nd R+ schedule: 1:5 praise

Generalization (**stimulus factors**): [people, place, materials, supervision, etc.] Vary staff, items presented (e.g., preferred and non-preferred foods, preferred and non-preferred toys), location, activities (e.g., snack, lunch, free play), fade staff proximity	Generalization (**response factors**): [rate, accuracy, magnitude, duration, etc.] Require clear responses (clear head nods/shakes), mix opportunities

Parametric details: Begin working on "no" items by selecting items the student dislikes. The communicative partner sits/ stands in front of the student, holds out the item and asks, "Do you want _____?" The prompter, standing behind the student should gently fully prompt him/her to shake his/her head no. If the student does not respond "no", never force them to eat the item - simply offer the item. When working on responding "yes", select items that you know the student really desires, using the same prompting strategy. As the student becomes more independent with responses, the prompter should gradually fade the amount of physical assistance needed and their proximity. Indicate prompt level required per response or + for independent responses. Start with "no" add "yes" and then intersperse opportunities for both.

Data Collection

Date	Communicative partner	Prompter	No	Yes	Item	Comments	

Response Key

Correct: +
Incorrect: -
No response: NR

100									
90									
80									
70									
60									
50									
40									
30									
20									
10									
Date									

Prompt Level Key

FP = full physical
PP = partial physical
M = model
G = gesture
PV = partial verbal
FV = full verbal

Pyramid Educational Consultants

Discrete Lesson Plan	Target Skill:	Responding "I don't know" (visually)

Student:	Teacher:	Date:

Behavior objective: When the student is asked a question that he/she does not know the answer, he/she will respond "I don't know" by exchanging a visual representation.
Functional association: Domain: Communication   Function: communication, independent living, social skills

Current lesson status [acquisition, fluency, maintenance]: acquisition
(trials/set; # data-points collected per week): 1-3 trials/set, 5 data points per week
Target Criterion (specify type of data: %, frequency, rate, duration, etc.): <1 prompt/5 trials, 3 staff

Current **Stimulus Control**: Needs a gesture to the written prompt "I don't know" in order to exchange it	Long-term **cue**: Novel activities/items and question
Discrete Trial format: Yes [maximum # per set] 3 trials/set	Sequential format: No Chained?: No

One vs. Two person prompt?: **One**	**Prompt Strategy**: Delayed Prompting *Pause interval (for hierarchy or delayed):* 1 second progressive time delay (max.5 secs.)

Error Correction: Built into procedure

Natural or additional completion R+: praise, small edible, gains information about unknown item	2nd R+ (during task): praise ("Super telling me that you don't know.")
Current 2nd R+ schedule: 1:1 praise, 1:1 small edible	Goal 2nd R+ schedule: 1:5 praise

Generalization (**stimulus factors**): [people, place, materials, supervision, etc.] Vary staff, questions asked, (e.g., "Where is ____?", "What is this?" (with an unfamiliar object) "Who made this?")	Generalization (**response factors**): [rate, accuracy, magnitude, duration, etc.] Ask questions that he/she does not know the answer, as well as questions which he/she does know the answer, vary number of questions asked at one time

Parametric details: At various times during the day, ask the student questions about his/her or other's activities that he/she does not know the answer. Begin with all known items, then introducing 10% unknown and gradually build to 50% known and 50% unknown. Begin teaching with a time delay of zero. Ask the question while simultaneously gesturing to the written phrase "I don't know." Record "+" if the student beats the prompt and independently exchanges the phrase and "-" if the student does not beat the prompt. For correct responses provide praise and label activity/item. Make sure to ask the student questions that he/she DOES know the answer to and praise the student for correctly responding to avoid over generalizing the "I don't know" response.

Data Collection

Date	Staff	Length of time delay	Beat the prompt?	Question	Activity/item (unknown)	Correct responses to known activities/items	Comments

Response Key		**Prompt Level Key**
Correct: + Incorrect: - No response: NR	100 / 90 / 80 / 70 / 60 / 50 / 40 / 30 / 20 / 10 / Date	FP = full physical PP = partial physical M = model G = gesture PV = partial verbal FV = full verbal

Discrete Lesson Plan	Target Skill:	Responding "I don't know"

Student:	Teacher:	Date:

Behavior objective: Throughout the day, the student will respond "I don't know" when asked to label unfamiliar objects.
Functional association: Domain: Communication　　　　Function: communication, social skills

Current lesson status [acquisition, fluency, maintenance]: acquisition
(trials/set; # data-points collected per week): 1-2 trials/set, disperse 4 sets/week, 5 data points per week
Target Criterion (specify type of data: %, frequency, rate, duration, etc.): 4/5 trials without prompting, 3 staff

Current **Stimulus Control**: Needs a model	Long-term **cue**: Novel objects and question

Discrete Trial format: Yes [maximum # per set] 2 trials/set	Sequential format: No Chained?: No

One vs. Two person prompt? **One**	**Prompt Strategy**: Delayed Prompting *Pause interval (for hierarchy or delayed):* 1 second progressive time delay (max.5 secs.)

Error Correction: Built into procedure

Natural or additional completion R+: praise, information	2nd R+ (during task): praise ("Great telling me that you don't know!")
Current 2nd R+ schedule: 1:1 praise	Goal 2nd R+ schedule: 1:2 praise

Generalization (**stimulus factors**): [people, place, materials, supervision, etc.] Vary staff, pictures and objects, work location, vary form of question (e.g., "What is this?", "Do you know what this is?") and activities	Generalization (**response factors**): [rate, accuracy, magnitude, duration, etc.] Vary number of trials per set, teach equivalent statements (e.g., "I've no clue!" "Can you tell me?")

Parametric details: Begin with all known items, then introduce 10% unknown items and gradually build to 50% known and 50% unknown. For example, show the student a picture or item that he/she is not familiar with (e.g., new item during circle or a new food item sent in his/her lunchbox) and ask, "What's this?" Begin teaching with a time delay of zero. After asking the question, immediately model "I don't know" for the student to imitate. After the student responds "I don't know" staff should provide praise and label the item. Continue to increase the time delay by one second increments after every 5 correct trials. Record "+" if the student beats the prompt and "-" if the student does not beat the prompt. Also, work on this skill throughout the day during activities such as cooking, arts/crafts, and structured playtime. Be sure to ask the student to identify objects that he/she does know so that the student does not over generalize the "I don't know" response.

Data Collection

Date	Staff	Length of time delay	Beat the prompt?	Item (unknown)	Correct response to known items	Comments

Response Key

Correct: +
Incorrect: -
No response: NR

100											
90											
80											
70											
60											
50											
40											
30											
20											
10											
Date											

Prompt Level Key

FP = full physical
PP = partial physical
M = model
G = gesture
PV = partial verbal
FV = full verbal

Pyramid Educational Consultants

Discrete Lesson Plan	Target Skill:	Answering questions about others' past events

Student:	Teacher:	Date:

Behavior objective: After others (e.g., peers) complete an activity(s)/event(s), the student will answer questions about what "they", "he", "she" just did.

Functional association: Domain: Communication   Function: memory skills, communication

Current lesson status [acquisition, fluency, maintenance]: acquisition
(trials/set; # data-points collected per week): 3 trials/set, 3 data points per week
Target Criterion (specify type of data: %, frequency, rate, duration, etc.): 80% of total opportunities, 10 situations, 6 staff

Current **Stimulus Control**: Needs verbal model	Long-term **cue**: Question about others past events
Discrete Trial format: Yes [maximum # per set] 3 trials/set	Sequential format: No Chained?: No

One vs. Two person prompt?: **One**	**Prompt Strategy**: Delayed Prompting *Pause interval (for hierarchy or delayed):* 1 second progressive time delay (max. 5 secs.)

Error Correction: Built into procedure

Natural or additional completion R+: praise, edible	2nd R+ (during task): praise ("Great job! That's right, they just finished playing basketball.")
Current 2nd R+ schedule: 1:1 praise, 1:1 edible	Goal 2nd R+ schedule:1:2 praise, fade edible
Generalization (**stimulus factors**): [people, place, materials, supervision, etc.] Vary staff, location, activities, people being commented on (e.g., teacher, classmates, students from other classrooms)	Generalization (**response factors**): [rate, accuracy, magnitude, duration, etc.] Vary the number of questions asked, ask more in depth questions about materials used and people seen, increase the delay between the event and the question

Parametric details: After the completion of an event by others, ask the student questions about what he/she just saw. Start with "What" questions. For example, "What did they just do?", "What did she just do?" etc. Ask the student the question just after the event has ended. Once the student is correct on 80% of total opportunities then begin to ask "Who" questions. For example, "Who played basketball?" Immediately after asking the question, verbally model the correct answer. Continue to increase the time delay by one-second increments after every 5 correct trials. Record a "+" if the student beats the prompt and "-" if the student does not beat the prompt. Because the trials per set indicates 3, this requires that the student be given the opportunity to respond to questions involving they, he and she, so mix them up. The time frame can be expanded so that activities can be arranged so all three responses are targeted and are considered a set.

Data Collection

Date	Staff	Activity/event	Type of question: what/who/where	Response: they/he/she	Length of delay	Beat the prompt?	Comments

Response Key		**Prompt Level Key**
Correct: + Incorrect: - No response: NR	(graph grid: 100, 90, 80, 70, 60, 50, 40, 30, 20, 10, Date)	FP = full physical PP = partial physical M = model G = gesture PV = partial verbal FV = full verbal

| Discrete Lesson Plan | Target Skill: | Responding to personal past events (visual) |

| Student: | Teacher: | Date: |

Behavior objective: After completing an activity or upon returning from a community outing, the student will answer the question, "What did you just do?"
Functional association: Domain: Communication   Function: memory skills, expressive communication

Current lesson status [acquisition, fluency, maintenance]: acquisition
(trials/set; # data-points collected per week): 1 trial/set, 3 data points per week
Target Criterion (specify type of data: %, frequency, rate, duration, etc.): 4/5 opportunities, 10 situations

| Current **Stimulus Control**: Needs full physical prompting to pick up picture | Long-term **cue**: Question about past personal event |

| Discrete Trial format: Yes [maximum # per set] 1 trial/set | Sequential format: No Chained?: No |

| One vs. Two person prompt?: **One** | **Prompt Strategy**: Delayed Prompting *Pause interval (for hierarchy or delayed):* 1 second progressive time delay (max. 5 secs.) |

Error Correction: Built into procedure

| Natural or additional completion R+: praise, edible | 2nd R+ (during task): praise ("Nice going! That's right, we did go to McDonalds.") |

| Current 2nd R+ schedule: 1:1 praise, 1:1 edible | Goal 2nd R+ schedule: 1:2 praise, |

| Generalization (**stimulus factors**): [people, place, materials, supervision, etc.] Vary staff, locations (e.g., food store, mall, or department store), activities | Generalization (**response factors**): [rate, accuracy, magnitude, duration etc.] Vary the number of questions asked, ask more in depth questions about materials used and people seen, increase delay between event and question |

Parametric details: After completing an activity (e.g., getting into the vehicle after a community outing), ask the student either what he/she just did or where he/she just went. Immediately physically (or gestural if effective) prompt the student to select the correct picture. Continue to increase the time delay by one second increments after every 5 correct trials. Record "+" if the student beats the prompt and "-" if the student does not beat the prompt. Staff should give a choice of 4 pictures.

Data Collection

Date	Staff	Location	Activity	Length of delay	Beat the prompt?	Comments	

Response Key		**Prompt Level Key**
Correct: + Incorrect: - No response: NR	100 / 90 / 80 / 70 / 60 / 50 / 40 / 30 / 20 / 10 / Date	FP = full physical PP = partial physical M = model G = gesture PV = partial verbal FV = full verbal

Discrete Lesson Plan	**Target Skill:**	**Using appropriate volume (request)**

Student:	Teacher:	Date:

Behavior objective: Throughout the school day, the student will use appropriate volume while making requests.
Functional association: Domain: Communication   Function: communication skills, independent living skills

Current lesson status [acquisition, fluency, maintenance]: acquisition
(trials/set; # data-points collected per week): 1-3 trials/set, 3 data points per week
Target Criterion (specify type of data: %, frequency, rate, duration, etc.): <1 prompt per 5 opportunities, 2 staff

Current **Stimulus Control**: Needs a model	Long-term **cue**: Item
Discrete Trial format: Yes [maximum # per set] 3 trials/set	Sequential format: No Chained?: No

One vs. Two person prompt?: **Two**	**Prompt Strategy**: Prompt Hierarchy- ignore, model, lose turn (e.g., move to back of line) Pause interval (for hierarchy or delayed): 5 seconds

Error Correction: Continued Prompt Hierarchy

Natural or additional completion R+: natural: gets access to item, praise	2nd R+ (during task): praise ("Nice asking loudly.")
Current 2nd R+ schedule: 1:1 praise	Goal 2nd R+ schedule: 1:5 praise
Generalization (**stimulus factors**): [people, place, materials, supervision, etc.] Vary staff, location (e.g., classroom, kitchen, fast food, cafeteria) items and activities (e.g., snack, lunch), reduce power of reinforcers requested, natural reactions to low volume (e.g., "What did you say?" "I can't understand you.")	Generalization (**response factors**): [rate, accuracy, magnitude, duration, etc.] Require louder requests

Parametric details: Create a situation in which the student needs something. If the request is too quiet, ignore it. If the student fails to repeat the request at an appropriate volume, the trainer should then model the request (at an audible level - e.g., "I want chips"). If he/she still does not make the request at an audible level, the trainer should move the student to the back of the line or go on to the next student. Begin with powerful reinforcers and then move to less motivating items. Note: the purpose of this lesson is to teach the student to use appropriate volume, so make sure student can imitate volume level and not just imitate named item.

Data Collection

Date	Communicative partner	Trainer	Situation	Level of prompt given	Phrase	Comments

Response Key		**Prompt Level Key**
Correct: + Incorrect: - No response: NR	100 90 80 70 60 50 40 30 20 10 Date	FP = full physical PP = partial physical M = model G = gesture PV = partial verbal FV = full verbal

Discrete Lesson Plan	Target Skill:	Use communication book when speech is not understood

Student:	Teacher:	Date:

Behavior objective: When a listener does not understand the student's speech, he/she will use his/her communication book to clarify his/her want or need..
Functional association: Domain: Communication   Function: communication , independent living skills, social skills

Current lesson status [acquisition, fluency, maintenance]: acquisition
(trials/set; # data-points collected per week): 1 trial/set, 3 data points per week
Target Criterion (specify type of data: %, frequency, rate, duration, etc.): <1 prompt/5 trials, 3 staff

Current **Stimulus Control**: Needs a gesture to book	Long-term **cue**: "I don't understand", shrugged shoulders

Discrete Trial format: Yes [maximum # per set] 1trial/set	Sequential format: No Chained?: No

One vs. Two person prompt?: **Two**	**Prompt Strategy**: Fading – FP, PF, G Pause interval (for hierarchy or delayed):

Error Correction: Use needed prompt level

Natural or additional completion R+: natural: having want/need understood (access), praise, small	2nd R+ (during task): praise: ("Great job using your communication book.")
Current 2nd R+ schedule: 1:1 praise 1:1 small edible	Goal 2nd R+ schedule: 1:5 praise

Generalization (**stimulus factors**): [people, place, materials, supervision, etc.] Vary staff, time of day, phrases that are "unintelligible" (e.g., work on this skill with a variety of phrases that the student says), vary the way you show that you do not understand his/her speech (e.g., "I don't understand", puzzled look on your face, shrug of shoulders), increase distance to staff	Generalization (**response factors**): [rate, accuracy, magnitude, duration, etc.]

Parametric details: If a student has a history with PECS and has some speech, but poor articulation the communication book should be used as a means of clarifying unintelligible speech. At various times during the day, act puzzled by the student's unintelligible verbal requests and/or comments. Respond by saying, "_____, I don't understand." The 2nd trainer immediately prompts the student to the communication book. The communicative partner rewards appropriate use of PECS and models the complete phrase. If the student imitates with improved articulation, provide praise. Either way, provide whatever was requested. Do not verbally prompt the student to "Go get your communication book", "Show me what you want." The 2nd trainer fades prompts and proximity.

Data Collection

Date	Trainer	Unintelligible speech	Staff Response (""What?" etc.)	Prompt	Comments

Response Key		**Prompt Level Key**
Correct: + Incorrect: - No response: NR	100 / 90 / 80 / 70 / 60 / 50 / 40 / 30 / 20 / 10 / Date	FP = full physical PP = partial physical M = model G = gesture PV = partial verbal FV = full verbal

Pyramid Educational Consultants

Discrete Lesson Plan	Target Skill:	Respond to 'wait'

Student:	Teacher :	Date:

Behavior objective: During specified times of the day, the student will wait to gain access to an item or activity.

Functional association: Domain: Communication   Function: follow instructions from others, social skills

Current lesson status [acquisition, fluency, maintenance]: acquisition
(trials/set; # data-points collected per week):1 trial per set, 3 per week
Target Criterion (specify type of data: %, frequency, rate, duration, etc.): <1prompt/3 minutes, across 4 items/activities

Current **Stimulus Control**: Given verbal direction, "You need to wait" paired with a "wait" card	Long-term **cue**: "Wait" card
Discrete Trial format: Yes [maximum # per set] 1 trial/set	Sequential format: No Chained?: No

One vs. Two person prompt?: **One**	Prompt Strategy : Shaping Pause interval (for hierarchy or delayed):

Error Correction: Decrease wait time interval on *NEXT* trial

Natural or additional completion R+: natural: access to item/activity	2nd R+ (during task): praise: ("Nice waiting.")
Current 2nd R+ schedule: 5 seconds/access, praise	Goal 2nd R+ schedule: 3 minutes/access, praise

Generalization (**stimulus factors**): [people, place, materials, supervision, etc.] Vary staff, locations, items (e.g., candy, pretzel, soda), activities (e.g., playground, cooking), increase staff proximity	Generalization (**response factors**): [rate, accuracy, magnitude, duration, etc.] Increase the amount of wait time

Parametric details: During specified structured times the following will occur: the student will request an item (e.g. popcorn), and staff will hand the wait card to the student and say, "Wait." After 1 second say, "Nice waiting", and remove the card from his/her hand and give access to the popcorn. After 3 trials of successful waiting (0 prompts), increase to 3 seconds. After 3 trials of successful waiting, continue to increase by 2 second increments until target time is met. The wait card can also be used at other times of the day (e.g., waiting for the bathroom, lunch, and an activity to begin). State the activity/item that the student waited for, the amount of wait time, and the number of prompts needed. The goal wait time is determined by 1 minute per year of age.

Data Collection

Date	Staff	Activity/ item	Wait time	# of prompts	Comments	

Response Key	100										**Prompt Level Key**
	90										
	80										
Correct: +	70										FP = full physical
Incorrect: -	60										PP = partial physical
No response: NR	50										M = model
	40										G = gesture
	30										PV = partial verbal
	20										FV = full verbal
	10										
	Date										

Community Lesson Plans

Discrete Lesson Plan	Target Skill:	Fasten seat belt

Student:	Teacher:	Date:

Behavior objective: Upon entering a car, the student will fasten his/her seat belt.

Functional association: Domain: Community   Function: safety

Current lesson status [acquisition, fluency, maintenance]: acquisition
(trials/set; # data-points collected per week): 1 set /week
Target Criterion (specify type of data: %, frequency, rate, duration, etc.): 4/5 trials without prompts

Current **Stimulus Control**: Full physical prompts	Long-term **cue**: Getting into a car
Discrete Trial format: No [maximum # per set]	Sequential format: Yes Chained?: Backward Chain

One vs. Two person prompt?: One	**Prompt Strategy**: Most to Least Prompt Hierarchy - FP, PP, G
	Pause interval (for hierarchy or delayed):

Error Correction: Backstep

Natural or additional completion R+: edible for fastening seat belt	2nd R+ (during task): praise, "Great job putting your seat belt on!"
Current 2nd R+ schedule: 1:1 praise for completing steps of the task independently, edible at end	Goal 2nd R+ schedule: praise at end of task, fade out edible
Generalization (**stimulus factors**): [people, place, materials, supervision, etc.] Vary staff, vehicles (e.g., school car, parent's car), type of seat belt (e.g., lap belt, shoulder/lap belt)	Generalization (**response factors**): [rate, accuracy, magnitude, duration, etc.]

Parametric details: Begin by fully prompting the student through all of the steps of the TA until the last step. Staff will begin by teaching this step first. Once the student has 3 correct trials on the target step, add teaching the second to last step to the sequence. Repeat this format until all steps are completed by the student independently.

Steps:											
1. Grasps the shoulder strap with hand											
2. Pulls strap across body											
3. Grasps the insert part of the belt with the other hand											
4. Inserts shoulder strap buckle into stationary end	.										
Total:											
Staff:											

Response Key												**Prompt Level Key**
	100											
	90											
	80											
Correct: +	70											FP = full physical
	60											PP = partial physical
Incorrect: -	50											M = model
No response: NR	40											G = gesture
	30											PV = partial verbal
	20											FV = full verbal
	10											
	Date											

Sequential Lesson Plan	Target Skill:	Retrieve items in grocery store	·

Student:	Teacher:	Date:

Behavior objective: When handed a picture of an item and given the verbal direction, "Get this" the student will get the specified item off of the grocery store shelf.
Functional association: Domain: Community   Function: grocery shopping skills

Current lesson status [acquisition, fluency, maintenance]: acquisition
(trials/set; # data-points collected per week): 1set/week
Target Criterion (specify type of data: %, frequency, rate, duration, etc.): 85% accurate, 3 staff, 10 items

Current **Stimulus Control**: Needs a gesture	Long-term **cue**: A picture grocery list
Discrete Trial format: No [maximum # per set]	Sequential format: Yes Chained?: Forward Chain

One vs. Two person prompt?: One	Prompt Strategy: Fading
	Pause interval (for hierarchy or delayed)

Error Correction: Backstep

Natural or additional completion R+: gets to buy and consume reinforcer after leaving the store	2nd R+ (during task): tokens, praise, "Great job getting the pop tart off the shelf!"
Current 2nd R+ schedule: 3 tokens, praise 1:1	Goal 2nd R+ schedule: 5 tokens 1:2, praise 1:3

Generalization (**stimulus factors**): [people, place, materials, supervision, etc.] Vary staff, locations (same store but in different location), and increase distance from student	Generalization (**response factors**): [rate, accuracy, magnitude, duration, etc.] Shop for longer periods of time, increase accuracy then increase rate

Parametric details: Begin with a list of 5 items. Give the student the picture of an item along with the verbal direction "Get this", then physically lead the child to the item on the shelf. After fully prompting this for 5 items across 3 outings, begin to fade prompts. As you fade your prompts, indicate the number of feet the student goes to retrieve an item, and whether the student retrieved the correct item.

Date	Staff	Location	Item	# feet	+/-	Comments

Response Key

Correct: +
Incorrect: -
No response: NR

100									
90									
80									
70									
60									
50									
40									
30									
20									
10									
Date									

Prompt Level Key

FP = full physical
PP = partial physical
M = model
G = gesture
PV = partial verbal
FV = full verbal

Pyramid Educational Consultants

Sequential Lesson Plan	Target Skill:	Stay with group

Student:	Teacher:	Date:

Behavior objective: When the student is in a store, he/she will stay with the group.

Functional association: Domain: Community   Function: safety, independence within the community

Current lesson status [acquisition, fluency, maintenance]: acquisition
(trials/set; # data-points collected per week): Data collected once a week
Target Criterion (specify type of data: %, frequency, rate, duration, etc.): < 2 prompts / 10 minutes / 3 staff

Current **Stimulus Control**: Needs hand held	Long-term **cue**: Shopping with a group

Discrete Trial format: No [maximum # per set]	Sequential format: Yes Chained?: No

One vs. Two person prompt?: **One**	**Prompt Strategy**: Graduated Guidance Pause interval (for hierarchy or delayed):

Error Correction: Backstep

Natural or additional completion R+: edible, praise	2nd R+ (during task): edible, praise ("Nice job staying with the group.")
Current 2nd R+ schedule: 1 edible:30 second/intermittent praise	Goal 2nd R+ schedule: 1 edible :2 minutes; 1:3 minutes social praise

Generalization (**stimulus factors**): [people, place, materials, supervision, etc.] Vary staff and locations (e.g., mall, grocery store, clothing), fade staff proximity	Generalization (**response factors**): [rate, accuracy, magnitude, duration, etc.] Increase amount of time in store

Parametric details: The student will stay with the group while in the store. The student must stay within 3 feet of staff. If he/she darts or moves farther away than 3 feet, Backstep the student to the last place he/she was with staff before leaving the area. Begin by walking in the store and then coming right out of the store. Immediately reinforce the student for staying with the group. Slowly increase the amount of time that you are in the store. Begin by staying for 30 seconds, and gradually increase to 1:30, 2:30, etc. Follow reinforcement schedule above. Indicate below the # prompts the student required to stay with the group.

Date	Staff	Location	# minutes in store	# prompts	Comments				

Response Key		**Prompt Level Key**

	100											
Correct: +	90											
Incorrect: -	80											
No response: NR	70											
	60											
	50											
	40											
	30											
	20											
	10											
	Date											

Response Key:
Correct: +
Incorrect: -
No response: NR

Prompt Level Key:
FP = full physical
PP = partial physical
M = model
G = gesture
PV = partial verbal
FV = full verbal

Discrete Lesson Plan	Target Skill:	Waiting in line at fast food restaurant

Student:	Teacher:	Date:

Behavior objective: At a fast food restaurant, the student will wait in line to order food.

Functional association: Domain: Community   Function: waiting

Current lesson status [acquisition, fluency, maintenance]: acquisition
(trials/set; # data-points collected per week): 1set/ week
Target Criterion (specify type of data: %, frequency, rate, duration, etc.): < 2 prompts/5 minutes, across 3 staff

Current **Stimulus Control**: Needs gesture	Long-term **cue**: A line at a fast food restaurant

Discrete Trial format: Yes [maximum # per set]	Sequential format: No Chained?: No

Two person One vs. prompt?: One	**Prompt Strategy**: Prompt Hierarchy - G, PP, FP Pause interval (for hierarchy or delayed): 3 seconds

Error Correction: Continued Prompt Hierarchy

Natural or additional completion R+: edible every 30 seconds for staying in line	2nd R+ (during task): praise, "Great job waiting in line!"
Current 2nd R+ schedule: edible every 30 seconds for appropriate waiting	Goal 2nd R+ schedule: edible every 2 minutes for appropriate waiting
Generalization (**stimulus factors**): [people, place, materials, supervision, etc.] Vary fast food restaurants, staff, increase staff proximity	Generalization (**response factors**): [rate, accuracy, magnitude, duration, etc.] Increase the amount of time the student has to wait in line, begin to go to sit down restaurants

Parametric details: Begin by **not** having the student wait in a line. Have him/her walk right up to the counter and order. Slowly begin to increase the amount of time the student has to wait, increasing by 1-minute increments. Reinforce every 30 seconds. State the length of time the student has to wait in line.

Date	Staff	Restaurant	Length of time	# prompts to wait	Comments

Response Key

Correct: +
Incorrect: -
No response: NR

100									
90									
80									
70									
60									
50									
40									
30									
20									
10									
Date									

Prompt Level Key

FP = full physical
PP = partial physical
M = model
G = gesture
PV = partial verbal
FV = full verbal

     Pyramid Educational Consultants

Sequential Lesson Plan	Target Skill:	Walk with cart in store

Student:	Teacher:	Date:

Behavior objective: When the student is in a store, he/she will hold onto the cart.

Functional association: Domain: Community   Function: independence within the community, safety

Current lesson status [acquisition, fluency, maintenance]: acquisition
(trials/set; # data-points collected per week): Data collected once a week
Target Criterion (specify type of data: %, frequency, rate, duration, etc.): < 2 prompts/15 minutes, across 3 staff

Current **Stimulus Control**: Needs full physical prompting	Long-term **cue**: Shopping in a store

Discrete Trial format: No [maximum # per set]	Sequential format: Yes Chained?: No

One vs. Two person prompt?: **One**	**Prompt Strategy**: Prompt Hierarchy - FP, PP, G Pause interval (for hierarchy or delayed): 3 seconds

Error Correction: Continued Prompt Hierarchy

Natural or additional completion R+: edible, praise	2nd R+ (during task): edible, praise ("Nice job holding onto the cart.")
Current 2nd R+ schedule: 1 edible:30 second, intermittent praise	Goal 2nd R+ schedule: 1 edible:2 minutes, 1:3 minutes social praise

Generalization (**stimulus factors**): [people, place, materials, supervision, etc.] Vary staff and locations (e.g., mall, grocery store, clothing), fade staff proximity	Generalization (**response factors**): [rate, accuracy, magnitude, duration, etc.] Increase amount of time in store

Parametric details: The student will hold onto the cart while in the store. If he/she lets go of the cart physically redirect him/her to hold onto it again. Follow prompt hierarchy stated above. Begin by staying in the store for 3 minutes. Once the student has < 2 prompts across 3 trials, increase the time to 5 minutes. Continue to increase the time once the student has 3 successful trials at each time interval.

Date	Staff	Location	# minutes in store	# prompts	Comments			

Response Key													**Prompt Level Key**
	100												
	90												
	80												
Correct: +	70												FP = full physical
	60												PP = partial physical
Incorrect: -	50												M = model
No response: NR	40												G = gesture
	30												PV = partial verbal
	20												FV = full verbal
	10												
	Date												

Domestic Lesson Plans

Sequential Lesson Plan	Target Skill:	Hang coat

Student:	Teacher:	Date:

Behavior objective: Upon entering the classroom, group home, or home, the student will hang his/her coat on a hook.

Functional association: Domain: Domestic   Function: independent living skills

Current lesson status [acquisition, fluency, maintenance]: acquisition
(trials/set; # data-points collected per week): 3 data points per week
Target Criterion (specify type of data: %, frequency, rate, duration, etc.): 90% of task analysis, 2 locations

Current **Stimulus Control**: Needs gestural to full physical prompting	Long-term **cue**: Entering (and staying in) a building, hooks available
Discrete Trial format: No [maximum # per set]	Sequential format: Yes Chained?: Backward Chain

One vs. Two person prompt?: **One**	**Prompt Strategy**: Most to Least Prompt Hierarchy - FP, PP, G
	Pause interval (for hierarchy or delayed):

Error Correction: Backstep (including for first step- back out the door!)

Natural or additional completion R+: natural: entering the room and access to next activity, praise, small edible	2nd R+ (during task): praise ("Great job pulling your sleeves out.")
Current 2nd R+ schedule: intermittent praise, small edible at completion of task	Goal 2nd R+ schedule: praise at completion of task only, (fade out edible)

Generalization (**stimulus factors**): [people, place, materials, supervision, etc.] Vary staff, location (e.g., classroom, group home, home), types of hooks (e.g., metal, plastic), types of coats (e.g. winter coats, spring jackets), fade staff proximity	Generalization (**response factors**): [rate, accuracy, magnitude, duration, etc.] Increase rate of completing the task

Parametric details: Full prompt through all steps until the last step. Teach this step using the prompt hierarchy. Once the student has completed this step 3 consecutive times independently, add prior step to the sequence. Allow the student to complete the remaining steps independently. Indicate level of prompt required.

Task Analysis Data Collection

Steps Date:										
1. Walks over to hook										
2. Pull sleeve #1 out										
3. Pull sleeve #2 out										
4. Holds coat by collar										
5. Hangs coat on hook										
Total:										
Staff:										

Response Key		**Prompt Level Key**
	100	
	90	
	80	
Correct: +	70	FP = full physical
Incorrect: -	60	PP = partial physical
	50	
No response: NR	40	M = model
	30	G = gesture
	20	PV = partial verbal
	10	FV = full verbal
	Date	

Sequential Lesson Plan	Target Skill:	**Prepare bowl of cereal**

Student:	Teacher:	Date:

Behavior objective: At scheduled times (e.g., breakfast and snack), the student will make a bowl of cereal.

Functional association: Domain: Domestic   Function: independent living skills

Current lesson status [acquisition, fluency, maintenance]: acquisition
(trials/set; # data-points collected per week): 3 data points per week
Target Criterion (specify type of data: %, frequency, rate, duration, etc.): 80% accuracy, across 2 staff, 3 different cereals

Current **Stimulus Control**: Needs full physical prompting	Long-term **cue**: Breakfast or snack time
Discrete Trial format: No [maximum # per set]	Sequential format: Yes Chained?: Backward Chain

One vs. Two person prompt? **One**	**Prompt Strategy**: Most to Least Prompt Hierarchy - FP, PP, G Pause interval (for hierarchy or delayed):

Error Correction: Provide sufficient prompt - increase support level next trial
         Anticipatory prompt for repeated errors on same step in sequence

Natural or additional completion R+: natural: eats cereal, praise	2nd R+ (during task): praise ("_____, great job getting the milk.")
Current 2nd R+ schedule: Intermittent praise	Goal 2nd R+ schedule: praise at completion of task

Generalization (**stimulus factors**): [people, place, materials, supervision, etc.] Vary staff, vary location (e.g., kitchen, classroom), types of cereals, bowls, and milk used, fade staff proximity for independent steps	Generalization (**response factors**): [rate, accuracy, magnitude, duration, etc.] Decrease time needed to complete task

Parametric details: Full prompt through all steps until the last step. Teach this step using the prompt hierarchy. Indicate the level of prompt necessary. Once the student completes this step independently for 3 consecutive trials, add the prior step to the sequence. Allow the student to complete the remaining steps independently.

Data Collection

Steps	Date:									
1. Get cereal										
2. Get milk										
3. Get bowl										
4. Get spoon										
5. Open cereal box										
6. Pour cereal into bowl										
7. Close cereal box										
8. Open milk										
9. Pour milk into bowl										
10. Close milk										
Total:										
Staff:										

Response Key	100												
	90												
	80												
Correct: +	70												
Incorrect: -	60												
No response: NR	50												
	40												
	30												
	20												
	10												
	Date												

Prompt Level Key

FP = full physical
PP = partial physical
M = model
G = gesture
PV = partial verbal
FV = full verbal

Sequential Lesson Plan	Target Skill:	Make cookies (slice and bake)	

Student:	Teacher:	Date:

Behavior objective: At scheduled times (e.g., before snacks and meals), the student will make refrigerated dough cookies.

Functional association: Domain: Domestic   Function: independent living skills

Current lesson status [acquisition, fluency, maintenance]: acquisition
(trials/set; # data-points collected per week): 1 data point per week
Target Criterion (specify type of data: %, frequency, rate, duration, etc.): 80% accuracy, across 2 staff, 2 kinds of cookies

Current **Stimulus Control**: Needs gestural to full physical prompting	Long-term **cue**: "Make cookies" as indicated on picture schedule

Discrete Trial format: No [maximum # per set]	Sequential format: Yes Chained?: Backward Chain (repeated)

One vs. Two person prompt?: **One**	**Prompt Strategy**: Most to Least Prompt Hierarchy - FP, PP, G Pause interval (for hierarchy or delayed):

Error Correction: Provide sufficient prompt - increase support level next trial

Natural or additional completion R+: Natural: eats cookies, praise	2nd R+ (during task): praise ("Great job getting the dough.")
Current 2nd R+ schedule: intermittent praise	Goal 2nd R+ schedule: praise at completion of task

Generalization (**stimulus factors**): [people, place, materials, supervision, etc.] Vary type of cookie dough (e.g., chocolate chip, peanut butter), vary staff, vary location (e.g., kitchen at group home, kitchen at school, kitchen at home), fade staff proximity	Generalization (**response factors**): [rate, accuracy, magnitude, duration, etc.] Vary number of cookies made (e.g., make enough for another class, too)

Parametric details: Staff will begin by cutting the end off the cookie dough wrapper. Staff will then physically prompt the student through the first three steps of the sequence. Staff will prompt the student to complete the last step of the sequence. Indicate what prompt level was needed to complete the target step. Once the student can complete this step 5 consecutive times independently, add the second to the last step to the sequence. Allow the student to complete the remaining step(s) independently. Once all the cookie dough is on the tray, staff will put the tray into the oven. When the cookies are done, the student gets to eat them.

Data Collection

Steps Date:										
1. Peel plastic from dough										
2. Pick up knife										
3. Cut off thin slice of dough										
4. Place slice on tray										
5. Repeat step 3 until all the dough is gone										
Total:										
Staff:										

Response Key	100											**Prompt Level Key**
	90											
	80											
Correct: +	70											FP = full physical
Incorrect: -	60											PP = partial physical
No response: NR	50											M = model
	40											G = gesture
	30											PV = partial verbal
	20											FV = full verbal
	10											
	Date											

Sequential Lesson Plan	Target Skill:	Make juice from powder mix

Student:	Teacher:	Date:

Behavior objective: Before snacks and meals, the student will make juice.
Functional association: Domain: Domestic   Function: independent living skills

Current lesson status [acquisition, fluency, maintenance]: fluency
(trials/set; # data-points collected per week): 3 data points per week
Target Criterion (specify type of data: %, frequency, rate, duration, etc.): 90% accuracy, across 2 staff

Current **Stimulus Control**: Prompting varies between gestural and full physical prompting	Long-term **cue**: "Make juice" as indicated on picture schedule
Discrete Trial format: No [maximum # per set]	Sequential format: Yes Chained?: Forward Chain

One vs. Two person prompt?: **One**	**Prompt Strategy**: Graduated Guidance across all steps Pause interval (for hierarchy or delayed):

Error Correction: Provide sufficient prompt (use anticipatory prompt for patterned errors)

Natural or additional completion R+: natural: drinks juice, praise	2nd R+ (during task): praise ("Great job filling up the pitcher.")
Current 2nd R+ schedule: praise 1:5 (praise every 5 steps)	Goal 2nd R+ schedule: praise at completion of task
Generalization (**stimulus factors**): [people, place, materials, supervision, etc.] Vary flavor of juice, pitchers, type of juice (e.g. can, packet), staff, location (e.g., kitchen, home, classroom), fade staff proximity for independent steps	Generalization (**response factors**): [rate, accuracy, magnitude, duration, etc.] Vary amount of juice made (e.g., make juice for another class too)

Parametric details: The student should gather materials upon cue, "make juice." Materials should be in a familiar place. Provide just enough prompting at each step to assure success. Indicate level of prompt needed to complete each step.

Task Analysis
1. Get juice pitcher	6. Fill up scoop with juice powder	11. Pick up spoon
2. Get big spoon	7. Empty juice powder into jug	12. Stir completely
3. Get juice	8. Turn on water	13. Put spoon in sink
4. Open juice container	9. Fill container completely	14. Replace top on juice container
5. Take out scoop	10. Turn off water	15. Put container on counter

Target Step	Date												
Total:													
Staff:													

Response Key

Correct: +
Incorrect: -
No response: NR

100									
90									
80									
70									
60									
50									
40									
30									
20									
10									
Date									

Prompt Level Key

FP = full physical
PP = partial physical
M = model
G = gesture
PV = partial verbal
FV = full verbal

Sequential Lesson Plan	Target Skill:	Make instant pudding from mix

Student:	Teacher:	Date:

Behavior objective: At scheduled times (e.g., before snacks and meals), the student will make pudding.

Functional association: Domain: Domestic   Function: independent living skills

Current lesson status [acquisition, fluency, maintenance]: acquisition
(trials/set; # data-points collected per week): 2 data points per week
Target Criterion (specify type of data: %, frequency, rate, duration, etc.): 80% accuracy, across 2 staff, 2 locations, 3 kinds of pudding

Current **Stimulus Control**: Needs gestural to full physical prompting	Long-term **cue**: "Make pudding" as indicated on picture schedule
Discrete Trial format: No [maximum # per set]	Sequential format: Yes Chained?: Forward Chain

One vs. Two person prompt?: **One**	**Prompt Strategy**: Graduated Guidance across all steps Pause interval (for hierarchy or delayed):

Error Correction: Provide sufficient prompt (use anticipatory prompt for patterned errors)

Natural or additional completion R+: Natural: eats pudding, praise	2nd R+ (during task): praise ("Great job getting the milk, ___.")
Current 2nd R+ schedule: intermittent praise	Goal 2nd R+ schedule: praise at completion of task

Generalization (**stimulus factors**): [people, place, materials, supervision, etc.] Vary type of pudding (e.g., brand, flavor), vary staff, vary location (e.g., kitchen, group home), fade staff proximity	Generalization (**response factors**): [rate, accuracy, magnitude, duration, etc.] Vary amount of pudding made (e.g., make enough for another day, too)

Parametric details: All of the needed materials will be on the table at the beginning of the activity. Use a container with a lid to make the pudding in because of step #6. Provide just enough prompting at each step to assure success. (If the pudding is being made by a group, set a timer for 5 seconds, so each child takes a turn shaking the container until the timer goes off.) Indicate level of prompt needed to complete each step.

Task Analysis Data Collection

Steps Date:										
1. Open box of mix										
2. Pour mix into container										
3. Measure 2 cups of milk										
4. Pour milk into container										
5. Put lid on container										
6. Shake the pudding										
7. Pass container to peer when the timer goes off (optional)										
Total:										
Staff:										

Response Key		**Prompt Level Key**
Correct: + Incorrect: - No response: NR	100 90 80 70 60 50 40 30 20 10 Date	FP = full physical PP = partial physical M = model G = gesture PV = partial verbal FV = full verbal

Sequential Lesson Plan	Target Skill:	Single place setting at table

Student:	Teacher:	Date:

Behavior objective: Given a placemat that contains visual cues (to be used as a model), the student will set his/her own place at the table.

Functional association: Domain: Domestic   Function: independent living skills, match to sample skills

Current lesson status [acquisition, fluency, maintenance]: acquisition
(trials/set; # data-points collected per week): 2 data points per week
Target Criterion (specify type of data: %, frequency, rate, duration, etc.): 90% accuracy, across 2 staff, 2 locations

Current **Stimulus Control**: Prompting level varies between gesture and full prompts	Long-term **cue**: "Set table" as indicated on picture schedule
Discrete Trial format: No [maximum # per set]	Sequential format: Yes Chained?: Backward Chain
One vs. Two person prompt?: **One**	**Prompt Strategy**: Most to Least Prompt Hierarchy - FP, PP, G Pause interval (for hierarchy or delayed):

Error Correction: Backstep if not on the target step

Natural or additional completion R+: natural: eats, praise	2nd R+ (during task): praise ("Nice job setting your place.")
Current 2nd R+ schedule: praise: 1:1 for items set out	Goal 2nd R+ schedule: praise at completion of setting his/her place
Generalization (**stimulus factors**): [people, place, materials, supervision, etc.] Vary staff, location (e.g., classroom, kitchen, group home, home), meals (e.g., breakfast, lunch, snack, dinner) and materials, fade staff proximity	Generalization (**response factors**): [rate, accuracy, magnitude, duration, etc.] Decrease time needed to complete task

Parametric details: The student will follow the steps outlined below. Fully prompt him/her through all the steps except the last one. Use the most-to-least prompt hierarchy to teach this step. Once the student has 3 consecutive correct responses, then add the second to last step to the sequence. Fully prompt to the second to last step, teach it, and then let the student finish the remaining steps independently.

Data Collection

Steps Date:										
1. Put place mat in front of chair										
2. Put plate/bowl on circle										
3. Place napkin										
4. Place fork										
5. Place knife										
6. Place spoon										
7. Place cup										
Total:										
Staff:										

Response Key	100											**Prompt Level Key**
	90											
	80											
Correct: +	70											FP = full physical
Incorrect: -	60											PP = partial physical
	50											
No response: NR	40											M = model
	30											G = gesture
	20											PV = partial verbal
	10											FV = full verbal
	Date											

Pyramid Educational Consultants

Sequential Lesson Plan	Target Skill:	Multiple place settings at table

Student:	Teacher:	Date:

Behavior objective: Before meals, the student will set the table.
Functional association: Domain: Domestic   Function: independent living skills

Current lesson status [acquisition, fluency, maintenance]: acquisition
(trials/set; # data-points collected per week): 2 data points per week
Target Criterion (specify type of data: %, frequency, rate, duration, etc.): 70% accuracy, 2 staff, 2 locations

Current **Stimulus Control**: Prompting level varies between gestures and full physical prompts	Long-term **cue** "Set table" as indicated on students picture schedule

Discrete Trial format: No [maximum # per set]	Sequential format: Yes Chained?: Backward Chain

One vs. Two person prompt?: **One**	**Prompt Strategy**: Most to Least Prompt Hierarchy - FP, PP, G Pause interval (for hierarchy or delayed):

Error Correction: Backstep if not on the target step

Natural or additional completion R+: natural: eats, praise	2nd R+ (during task): praise ("Nice job setting the table.")
Current 2nd R+ schedule: praise, 1:2 items set out	Goal 2nd R+ schedule: praise, 1:7 items set out
Generalization (**stimulus factors**): *[people, place, materials, supervision, etc.]* Vary staff, meals (e.g., breakfast, lunch), type of plates/silverware, staff proximity, location (e.g., classroom)	Generalization (**response factors**):*[rate, accuracy, magnitude, duration, etc.]* Vary number (maximum of 6) of place settings to be set, decrease time to set table

Parametric details: All of the materials needed will be lined up on the counter. Staff will complete all of the steps of the task analysis except the last step. The student will be shown a picture of "set table" and then prompted to complete the target step. Use the prompt hierarchy for teaching this step. Once the student has 3 correct responses on the target step, add the second to the last step to the sequence. The student should complete the remaining step(s) independently.

Task Analysis Data Collection

Steps Date:										
1. Put placemat in front of chair #1										
2. Put placemat in front of chair #2										
3. Put plate/ bowl on placemat #1										
4. Put plate/ bowl on placemat #2										
5. Put napkin on placemat #1										
6. Put napkin on placemat #2										
7. Put fork on napkin #1										
8. Put fork on napkin #2										
9. Put knife to right of plate/bowl #1										
10. Put knife to right of plate/bowl #2										
11. Put spoon to right of knife #1										
12. Put spoon to right of knife #2										
13. Place cup above the plate/bowl #1										
14. Place cup above the plate/bowl #2										
Total:										

Response Key

Correct: +
Incorrect: -
No response: NR

100									
90									
80									
70									
60									
50									
40									
30									
20									
10									
Date									

Prompt Level Key

FP = full physical
PP = partial physical
M = model
G = gesture
PV = partial verbal
FV = full verbal

Recreation/Leisure Lesson Plans

Discrete Lesson Plan	Target Skill:	Extending independent recreation/leisure skills

Student:	Teacher:	Date:

Behavior objective: At scheduled times, the student will engage in a variety of independent recreation/leisure activities.

Functional association: Domain: Recreation/Leisure   Function: time on task, independent recreation/leisure skills

Current lesson status [acquisition, fluency, maintenance]: fluency
(trials/set; # data-points collected per week): 3 data points per week
Target Criterion (specify type of data: %, frequency, rate, duration, etc.): <1 prompt/10 minutes, staff proximity 5-10 ft, 6 activities

Current **Stimulus Control**: Currently plays for up to two minutes with various toys, needs gestures to materials and penny card to continue on task	Long-term **cue**: Recreation/leisure activity on schedule
Discrete Trial format: Yes *[maximum # per set]*	Sequential format: No Chained?: No

One vs. Two person prompt?: **One**	**Prompt Strategy**: Shaping (NO prompts - reinforce criteria matching performance) *Pause interval (for hierarchy or delayed):*

Error Correction: One reminder to continue playing per activity

Natural or additional completion R+: praise, cashes out when has 5 tokens, continues with activity/access to next	2nd R+ (during task): praise ("Great building with your legos."), tokens
Current 2nd R+ schedule: praise, 1 token ARRT VI- 5 minutes	Goal 2nd R+ schedule: praise, 1 token ARRT VI- 7 minutes

Generalization (**stimulus factors**): *[people, place, materials, etc.]* Vary staff, locations and activities	Generalization (**response factors**): *[rate, accuracy, magnitude, duration, supervision, etc.]* Fade staff proximity, increase leisure time up to 10 minutes

Parametric details: During recreation/leisure time (e.g. puzzle, walkman, legos, parquetry blocks, computer game) staff will make items easily accessible to the student. Begin with a two-minute interval. One reminder to continue playing per activity is permitted. When the student meets criteria, increase the interval by 1 minute. Continue this procedure until the target time is met and the student is maintaining criteria. List the activity, length of time (duration) and the number of prompts needed for the student to stay engaged.

Data Collection

Date	Staff	Activity	Duration	Prompts	Staff Proximity	Comments	

Response Key

Correct: +
Incorrect: -
No response: NR

100										
90										
80										
70										
60										
50										
40										
30										
20										
10										
Date										

Prompt Level Key

FP = full physical
PP = partial physical
M = model
G = gesture
PV = partial verbal
FV = full verbal

Sequential Lesson Plan	Target Skill:	Playing a computer game

Student:	Teacher:	Date:

Behavior objective: During recreation/leisure time, the student will play a computer game.
Functional association: Domain: Recreation/Leisure   Function: independent leisure skills, time on task, fine motor skills

Current lesson status [acquisition, fluency, maintenance]: acquisition
(trials/set; # data-points collected per week): 2 data points per week
Target Criterion (specify type of data: %, frequency, rate, duration, etc.): 80% of T.A. across 2 staff/3 games, 10 minutes

Current **Stimulus Control**: Needs gestures to full physical prompts (level varies from step to step)	Long-term **cue**: "Computer" as indicated on picture schedule
Discrete Trial format: No *[maximum # per set]*	Sequential format: Yes Chained?: Forward Chain

One vs. Two person prompt?: **One**	**Prompt Strategy**: Graduated Guidance across all steps *Pause interval (for hierarchy or delayed):*

Error Correction: Provide sufficient prompt level (use anticipatory prompt for patterned errors)

Natural or additional completion R+: praise, continues game or access to next activity	2nd R+ (during task): praise ("Great job playing the computer game!"), tokens
Current 2nd R+ schedule: intermittent praise, 1 token VI-3 minutes for appropriate playing	Goal 2nd R+ schedule: praise and 1 token VI-5 minutes for appropriate playing
Generalization (**stimulus factors**): *[people, place, materials, etc.]* Vary staff, computer, games, location	Generalization (**response factors**): *[rate, accuracy, magnitude, duration, supervision, etc.]* Increase the amount of time on computer, fade staff proximity

Parametric details: When "computer" is indicated on the students picture schedule, he/she will go to the computer, sit down, and ask for help to turn it on. The student can then choose the desired computer game. This lesson is for the student who still requires some assistance accessing the desired computer game and also requires some prompting from staff in order to play.

Task Analysis Data Collection

Steps Date:										
1. Goes to the computer										
2. Sits down										
3. Asks for help to set up game										
4. Waits while game is being set up without touching keys										
5. Pushes appropriate keys to start program										
6. Pushes appropriate keys to continue program										
Total # of prompts:										
Duration:										
Game played:										
Total:										
Staff:										

Response Key	100											**Prompt Level Key**
	90											
	80											
Correct: +	70											FP = full physical
Incorrect: -	60											PP = partial physical
No response: NR	50											M = model
	40											
	30											G = gesture
	20											PV = partial verbal
	10											FV = full verbal
	Date											

Pyramid Educational Consultants

Sequential Lesson Plan	Target Skill:	Puzzle assembly

Student:	Teacher:	Date:

Behavior objective: During recreation/leisure time, the student will assemble puzzles.
Functional association: Domain: Recreation/leisure   Function: independent play skills, time on task

Current lesson status [acquisition, fluency, maintenance]: acquisition
(trials/set; # data-points collected per week): 2 data points per week
Target Criterion (specify type of data: %, frequency, rate, duration, etc.): completes 12 piece puzzle<1 prompt, across 4 puzzles

Current **Stimulus Control**: Needs gestures to full physical prompts to complete puzzles	Long-term **cue**: "Puzzles" as indicated on picture schedule
Discrete Trial format: No *[maximum # per set]*	Sequential format: Yes Chained?: Yes, but order can change

One vs. Two person prompt?: **One**	**Prompt Strategy**: Most to Least Prompt Hierarchy - FP, PP, G *Pause interval (for hierarchy or delayed):*

Error Correction: Provide sufficient prompt level

Natural or additional completion R+: praise, cashes out 3 tokens for small edible or activity of choice (cash-out should coincide with completion of a puzzle), completed puzzle	2nd R+ (during task): praise ("Great working on your puzzle."), cashes out 3 tokens for small edible or activity of choice (cash-out should coincide with completion of a puzzle)
Current 2nd R+ schedule: intermittent praise, earns 1 token VI-3 min for appropriate working	Goal 2nd R+ schedule: praise and earns 1 token VI-5 min. for appropriate working
Generalization (**stimulus factors**): *[people, place, materials, etc.]* Vary staff, work location and puzzles	Generalization (**response factors**): *[rate, accuracy, magnitude, duration, supervision, etc.]* Fade staff proximity, increase completion rate, increase # pieces

Parametric details: When "puzzle" is indicated on his/her picture schedule, the student will get a puzzle from the shelf. When he/she is working on a new puzzle, staff should take out one or two pieces, and then have the student complete the puzzle. Once the student is doing well with putting a few pieces in, then leave the outside pieces intact and have the student complete the inside pieces. When the student is independent with this, begin with just a few outside pieces intact, and have the student complete the puzzle. The last step is having the student complete the entire puzzle.

Data Collection

Date	Staff	Puzzle title	# pieces	# pieces independent	% Independent	Comments

Response Key	100										**Prompt Level Key**
	90										
	80										
Correct: +	70										FP = full physical
Incorrect: -	60										PP = partial physical
No response: NR	50										M = model
	40										G = gesture
	30										PV = partial verbal
	20										FV = full verbal
	10										
	Date										

Discrete Lesson Plan	**Target Skill:**	**Insert puzzle**

Student:	Teacher:	Date:

Behavior objective: During recreation/leisure or indoor recess, the student will complete insert puzzles.
Functional association: Domain: Recreation/Leisure   Function: independent play skills

Current lesson status [acquisition, fluency, maintenance]: acquisition
(trials/set; # data-points collected per week): 1 puzzle/set, 3-5 data points per week
Target Criterion (specify type of data: %, frequency, rate, duration, etc.): <1prompt/3 puzzles, 3 staff, 5 insert puzzles

Current **Stimulus Control**: Needs full physical prompting	Long-term **cue:** Chooses puzzle as preferred activity

Discrete Trial format: Yes	Sequential format: No
[maximum # per set] 1 puzzle/set	Chained?: No

One vs. Two person prompt?	**Prompt Strategy**: Delayed Prompting
One	*Pause interval (for hierarchy or delayed):* 1 second progressive time delay (max. 5 sec.)

Error Correction: Built into procedure

Natural or additional completion R+: earns 5 tokens towards trade in, praise	2nd R+ (during task): praise ("Great job working on your puzzle!"), tokens
Current 2nd R+ schedule: 1 token:1piece inserted, 1:1 praise	Goal 2nd R+ schedule: 1 token:1 puzzle completed, 1 praise:3 pieces inserted

Generalization (**stimulus factors**): *[people, place, materials, etc.]* Vary staff, location, puzzles	Generalization (**response factors**): *[rate, accuracy, magnitude, duration, supervision, etc.]* Vary number of puzzles, vary number of pieces in each puzzle, fade staff proximity

Parametric details: Begin teaching using a 5 piece insert puzzle. Start with a time delay of zero by immediately prompting the student to the correct placement of the target piece. As the student's skill indicates, gradually increase the time delay by 1 second increments until the student is successfully beating the prompt. Provide a variety of insert puzzles for the student to complete.

Data Collection

Date	Staff	Puzzle	Number of pieces	Time delay	Beat the prompt?	Comments

Response Key	100										**Prompt Level Key**
	90										
	80										
Correct: +	70										FP = full physical
Incorrect: -	60										PP = partial physical
No response: NR	50										M = model
	40										G = gesture
	30										PV = partial verbal
	20										FV = full verbal
	10										
	Date										

Pyramid Educational Consultants

Discrete Lesson Plan	Target Skill:	Using a "choice" board

Student:	Teacher:	Date:

Behavior objective: When "choose" is indicated on the student's picture schedule, he/she will use his/her "choice" board to select a recreation/leisure activity.
Functional association: Domain: Recreation/Leisure   Function: independent recreation/leisure skills, making choice

Current lesson status [acquisition, fluency, maintenance]: acquisition
(trials/set; # data-points collected per week): 2 data points per week
Target Criterion (specify type of data: %, frequency, rate, duration, etc.): <1 prompt/5 trials, 3 staff

Current **Stimulus Control**: Needs a gesture to "choice" board	Long-term **cue**: "Choose" indicated on picture schedule

Discrete Trial format: Yes *[maximum # per set]* 1	Sequential format: No Chained?: No

One vs. Two person prompt?: **One**	**Prompt Strategy**: Delayed Prompting *Pause interval (for hierarchy or delayed):* 1 second progressive time delay

Error Correction: Built into procedure

Natural or additional completion R+: natural: preferred activity, praise, opportunity to earn R+ during chosen task	2nd R+ (during task): praise: ("Nice job using your "choice" board!")
Current 2nd R+ schedule: 1:1 praise	Goal 2nd R+ schedule: 1:5 praise

Generalization (**stimulus factors**): *[people, place, materials, etc.]* Vary staff, time of day, items available on "choice" board	Generalization (**response factors**): *[rate, accuracy, magnitude, duration, supervision, etc.]* Fade staff proximity

Parametric details: The student knows how to use the "choice" board but currently will not go to it independently. Once he/she goes to the board, he/she is independent with the rest of the task. Once the student sees "choose" on his/her picture schedule, begin teaching with a time delay of zero by immediately gesturing to the "choice" board. The choice board should be located in close proximity to the picture schedule (e.g. hanging on the wall next to the schedule). Increase the time delay to one second when the student follows the gesture for five consecutive trials. Trials need to be dispersed throughout the day. Continue to increase the time delay by one second after five successful consecutive trials. Record "+" if the student beats the prompt and "-" if he/she does not beat the prompt.

Data Collection

Date	Staff	Length of time delay	Beat the prompt? "+" or "-"	Trainer	Comments		

Response Key	100											**Prompt Level Key**
	90											
	80											
Correct: +	70											FP = full physical
	60											PP = partial physical
Incorrect: -	50											
	40											M = model
No response: NR	30											G = gesture
	20											PV = partial verbal
	10											FV = full verbal
	Date											

School-Based Lesson Plans

Discrete Lesson Plan	Target Skill:	Counting: 1:1 correspondence with template

Student:	Teacher:	Date:

Behavior objective: During specified activities (e.g. snack), the student will count out a predetermined number of items.
Functional association: Domain: School Based   Function: money skills, purchasing skills, following directions

Current lesson status [acquisition, fluency, maintenance]: acquisition
(trials/set; # data-points collected per week): 5 trials/set, 10 data points per week
Target Criterion (specify type of data: %, frequency, rate, duration, etc.): 85% accuracy, #'s 1-5 with number in view

Current **Stimulus Control**: Needs gestural prompting	Long-term **cue**: Items and instructional cue

Discrete Trial format: Yes [maximum # per set] 5 trials/set	Sequential format: No Chained?: No

One vs. Two person prompt?: One	**Prompt Strategy**: Delayed Prompting (between verbal cue and visual dots) *Pause interval (for hierarchy or delayed):* 1 second progressive time delay (max. 5 sec.)

Error Correction: Built into procedure (if error, decrease interval next trial)

Natural or additional completion R+: earns 4 tokens toward cash out	2nd R+ (during task): praise (" Nice job counting out the spoons!"), token
Current 2nd R+ schedule: 1:1 praise, ARRT VI 3 min. 3 tokens	Goal 2nd R+ schedule: 1:4 praise, ARRT VI 3 min. 5 tokens

Generalization (**stimulus factors**): [people, place, materials, supervision, etc.] Vary staff, materials (e.g., goldfish, macaroni for project, cups for breakfast), locations (e.g., kitchen, other classrooms), flashcards with the #'s on them, fade staff proximity	Generalization (**response factors**): [rate, accuracy, magnitude, duration, etc.] Provide directions which involve more than one number (e.g., "Take 4 goldfish and 2 jellybeans.")

Parametric details: During functional/relevant activities, such as art projects, playtime, snack, and breakfast, give the student directions that involve counting. For example, the student requests goldfish and you say ,"Take 3 goldfish." The student will take the goldfish and place them on a template, which contains the target number and the corresponding number of dots. After the student has counted them out, he/she can eat them. Begin by giving the direction and simultaneously physically prompting the student to take the directed number of items and place them on the dots. The dots are visual cues that will have to be systematically faded later. As soon as the student is 80% accurate with the target number, begin to fade (reduce) the size of the dots until they are gone. Fading the dots can be done in a series of 4 -5 steps depending on the student (e.g. 3/4 size, 1/2 size, 1/4 size etc.).

Data Collection

Date	Staff	Time delay	Beat the prompt?	Number and dots	Dot size	Number only	Comments

Response Key		**Prompt Level Key**
Correct: + Incorrect: - No response: NR	100 / 90 / 80 / 70 / 60 / 50 / 40 / 30 / 20 / 10 / Date	FP = full physical PP = partial physical M = model G = gesture PV = partial verbal FV = full verbal

Discrete Lesson Plan	Target Skill:	Counting/graphing

Student:	Teacher:	Date:

Behavior objective: At scheduled times, the student will count items and complete a graph.
Functional association: Domain: School Based   Function: counting skills, discrimination skills, graphing skills

Current lesson status [acquisition, fluency, maintenance]: acquisition for graphing, **fluency for counting**
(trials/set; # data-points collected per week): 5-10 trials/set, 10-20 data points per week
Target Criterion (specify type of data: %, frequency, rate, duration, etc.): 80% accuracy for counting/graphing, 3 different
sets of materials to graph

Current **Stimulus Control**: Needs a model	Long-term **cue**: Schedule cue, objects to count/graph

Discrete Trial format: Yes	Sequential format: No
[maximum # per set] 5-10/set, disperse 3 sets across week	Chained?: No

One vs. Two person prompt?	Prompt Strategy: Model
One	Pause interval (for hierarchy or delayed):

Error Correction: 4-step switch

Natural or additional completion R+: praise, earns 5 tokens towards trade in	2nd R+ (during task): praise ("Very nice graphing!"), tokens
Current 2nd R+ schedule: 1:1 praise, 1:1 token	Goal 2nd R+ schedule: 1:2 praise and token

Generalization (**stimulus factors**): [people, place, materials, supervision, etc.] Vary items and pictures, vary graphing materials (e.g. crayons, markers) vary staff, locations, vary questions (e.g. "How many _____ do you see?" or "Graph the number of umbrellas."), fade staff proximity	Generalization (**response factors**): [rate, accuracy, magnitude, duration, etc.] Vary number of trials per set, vary task (e.g. "Graph the number of green books and the number of red books."), increase task completion rate

Parametric details: Give a picture with a variety of items on it or give a group of objects and ask "How many _____?" The question should require the student to discriminate by color, shape, and size. After the student counts the objects he/she should color in a block on the graph to represent each one. Indicate "+" for each graph completed correctly and independently or score a "-" if the student needs a model. To aid generalization, work on this skill during group activities, based on the unit of the week, the weather, or a trip to the library.

Data Collection

Date	Staff	How many?	Graph	How many?	Graph	How many?	Graph	Comments

Response Key	100											**Prompt Level Key**
	90											
	80											
Correct: +	70											FP = full physical
Incorrect: -	60											PP = partial physical
No response: NR	50											M = model
	40											G = gesture
	30											PV = partial verbal
	20											FV = full verbal
	10											
	Date											

Pyramid Educational Consultants

Sequential Lesson Plan	Target Skill:	Cut with scissors

Student:	Teacher:	Date:

Behavior objective: During structured activities, the student will cut out shapes with scissors.
Functional association: Domain: School Based   Function: fine motor skills

Current lesson status [acquisition, fluency, maintenance]: acquisition
(trials/set; # data-points collected per week): 4 trials/set, 2 data points per week
Target Criterion (specify type of data: %, frequency, rate, duration, etc.): 4/5 independent opportunities across 4 shapes

Current **Stimulus Control**: Needs full physical prompting	Long-term **cue**: Items for project/product, scissors

Discrete Trial format: No [maximum # per set] 10 trials/set	Sequential format: Yes Chained?: No

One vs. Two person prompt?: **One**	**Prompt Strategy**: Fading (FP, PP, G, +) Pause interval (for hierarchy or delayed):

Error Correction: Use level of assistance needed

Natural or additional completion R+: praise, use of objects/shapes cut out, tokens	2nd R+ (during task): praise ("Terrific job cutting out the shape."), tokens
Current 2nd R+ schedule: 1:1 (shape) token, 5 tokens toward cash out, intermittent praise	Goal 2nd R+ schedule: 1:3 (shapes) token, praise after each cut out shape

Generalization (**stimulus factors**): [people, place, materials, supervision, etc.] Vary staff, material (e.g. construction paper, tissue paper, clay), vary color and width of outlined shapes, location, scissors, projects, and fade staff proximity	Generalization (**response factors**): [rate, accuracy, magnitude, duration, etc.] Increase the rate at which the student cuts, increase number of pieces cut per set

Parametric details: During structured activities such as playing with clay or arts and crafts time, the student will cut out shapes. Begin by teaching squares. The shapes to be cut will be outlined with a black medium tip marker. Indicate to the student that "we need to do some cutting for our project". Begin by fully prompting the student to cut out the shapes. Slowly decrease the amount of physical prompting you need to give. Indicate prompt level used below. Once the student meets criteria with squares, teach triangles, rectangles, diamonds, stars and circles, introducing one new shape once criteria is met on the target shape.

Data Collection

Date	Staff	Shape	Prompt level	Comments

Response Key		**Prompt Level Key**
Correct: + Incorrect: - No response: NR	100 90 80 70 60 50 40 30 20 10 Date	FP = full physical PP = partial physical M = model G = gesture PV = partial verbal FV = full verbal

Sequential Lesson Plan	Target Skill:	Describe order of events

Student:	Teacher:	Date:

Behavior objective: At the completion of an obstacle course activity, the student will answer what came first, next and last.
Functional association: Domain: School based   Function: sequencing skills, conceptual skills

Current lesson status [acquisition, fluency, maintenance]: fluency
(trials/set; # data-points collected per week):10-15 data points per week
Target Criterion (specify type of data: %, frequency, rate, duration, etc.): 85% accuracy, 3 staff, 3 activities

Current **Stimulus Control**: Needs a visual cue	Long-term **cue**: Actions plus first, next, last question

Discrete Trial format: No [maximum # per set]	Sequential format: Yes Chained?: No

One vs. Two person prompt? **One**	**Prompt Strategy**: Delayed Prompting *Pause interval (for hierarchy or delayed):* 1 second progressive time delay (max. 5 sec.)

Error Correction: Built into procedure (decrease interval on next trial)

Natural or additional completion R+: praise, continues/completes activity	2nd R+ (during task): praise ("Great job telling what happened first, _____!"), earns 5 tokens towards trade in
Current 2nd R+ schedule: 1:1 praise and token	Goal 2nd R+ schedule: 1:4 praise and token

Generalization (**stimulus factors**): [people, place, materials, supervision, etc.] Vary staff, activities worked on, location, materials (e.g. actions, pictures, directions), vary order of questions (e.g. begin with "What was the last thing you did?" or "What happened second?")	Generalization (**response factors**): [rate, accuracy, magnitude, duration, etc.] Vary trials per set, have the student describe the whole sequence of actions/activities beginning sentences with the words "first", "next, and "last", work on the words "first", "second, "third", incorporate into other functional activities

Parametric details: At the completion of the obstacle course, ask the student "What happened first?", "What happened next?", and "What happened last?" Have pictures of the actions that the student performed with a few distracters available as visual cues. When you ask the question, simultaneously point to the correct picture. The student will pick up the picture and place it on the first square of his/her card, indicating "first". Continue this sequence until all 3 squares are complete. Other functional activities could include: during the game "Simon Says", sequencing motor acts (e.g. clap, stomp, jump), or sequencing steps within a functional routine (e.g. stand up, get coat, go to the door). Begin teaching using 0 time delay for all 3 questions. Also, indicate time delay used below under the appropriate column or if prompt was beaten (+/-).

Data Collection

Date	Staff	First	Next	Last	Activity	Beat the prompt?	Comments

Response Key

Correct: +
Incorrect: -
No response: NR

100										
90				-						
80										
70										
60										
50										
40										
30										
20										
10										
Date										

Prompt Level Key

FP = full physical
PP = partial physical
M = model
G = gesture
PV = partial verbal
FV = full verbal

Discrete Lesson Plan	Target Skill:	Get named objects

Student:	Teacher:	Date:

Behavior objective: During functional situations, the student will obtain requested objects.
Functional association: Domain: School Based   Function: direction following

Current lesson status [acquisition, fluency, maintenance]: acquisition
(trials/set; # data-points collected per week): 1-2 trial/set, 2 data points per object per week
Target Criterion (specify type of data: %, frequency, rate, duration, etc.): 10 objects, 75% accurate, 2 staff

Current **Stimulus Control**: Needs an identical visual object	Long-term **cue**: Objects and directions

Discrete Trial format: Yes [maximum # per set] 1-2 trial/set	Sequential format: No Chained?: No

One vs. Two person prompt?: **One**	**Prompt Strategy**: Delayed Prompting *Pause interval (for hierarchy or delayed)*: 1 second progressive time delay (max. 5 sec.)

Error Correction: Built into procedure (if error, decrease interval on next trial)

Natural or additional completion R+: natural (use of object obtained), praise	2nd R+ (during task): praise (" Nice job taking the fork.")
Current 2nd R+ schedule: praise following correct response	Goal 2nd R+ schedule: praise after every 3 correct responses

Generalization (**stimulus factors**): [people, place, materials, supervision, etc.] Vary staff, items (e.g., different forks, spoons), locations (e.g. cafeteria, gym, music), situations, directions given (e.g., "Take the spoon.", " Get the knife.")	Generalization (**response factors**): [rate, accuracy, magnitude, duration, etc.] Increase the number of objects retrieved, incorporate into daily or task routine schedule

Parametric details: During structured activities, staff will ask the student to, "Take the ____." or "Get the ____." Staff will ask these questions during functional activities, such as breakfast, playtime, or clean up. For example, during breakfast hold out a spoon and a fork and ask the student to, "Take the spoon." The student will need the spoon to eat his/her cereal. Another example might be asking the student to, "Take the towel" as you hold out a towel and a toy after the student completes hand washing. At least 2 items will be in view when asking the question. Initially, contextual cues are used to aid the students success, however, they will need to be faded as the students repertoire increases. Probe incorporating objects into either a daily or task routine schedule to see if the child is able to follow the object direction independent of contextual cues and in the absence of items being presented. Note that this lesson is done independent of picture based direction following.

Data Collection

Date	Staff	Object	Direction given	Time delay	Beat the prompt?	Comments

Response Key

Correct: +
Incorrect: -
No response: NR

100										
90										
80										
70										
60										
50										
40										
30										
20										
10										
Date										

Prompt Level Key

FP = full physical
PP = partial physical
M = model
G = gesture
PV = partial verbal
FV = full verbal

Discrete Lesson Plan	Target Skill:	Follow directions with spatial concepts

Student:	Teacher:	Date:

Behavior objective: During activities, such as "Hide and Seek", "Simon Says", and "Follow the Leader", the student will follow directions involving spatial concepts.
Functional association: Domain: School Based   Function: following directions involving prepositions

Current lesson status [acquisition, fluency, maintenance]: fluency
(trials/set; # data-points collected per week): 5 trials/set, 10 data points/week
Target Criterion (specify type of data: %, frequency, rate, duration, etc.): 4/5 opportunities w/o prompting , 4 concepts
(in front, in back, under, next to)

Current **Stimulus Control**: Needs gestural prompting	Long-term **cue**: Spatial direction
Discrete Trial format: Yes [maximum # per set] 5 trials/set	Sequential format: No Chained?: No

One vs. Two person prompt?: **One**	**Prompt Strategy**: Delayed Prompting *Pause interval (for hierarchy or delayed):* 1 second progressive time delay (max. 5 sec.)

Error Correction: Built into procedure (if error occurs, decrease interval next trial)

Natural or additional completion R+: 5 tokens earned toward cash out, access to next activity, obtains items	2nd R+ (during task): praise (" Great job following directions!")
Current 2nd R+ schedule: 1:3 (token/direction), 1:4 praise	Goal 2nd R+ schedule: 1:5 (token/direction), 1:5 praise

Generalization (**stimulus factors**): [people, place, materials, supervision, etc.] Vary staff, locations, items, activities, direction statements given (e.g. "Look in back of the couch.", "Get the toy from under the chair.")	Generalization (**response factors**): [rate, accuracy, magnitude, duration, etc.] Increase the number of directions followed, interchange "behind" for "in back", "beside" for "next to", begin to have the student be the leader and give the directions

Parametric details: During activities such as, "Hide and seek", "Follow the leader" or "Simon Says", have the student follow directions involving spatial concepts. Initially, have the student retrieve/find items that are reinforcing. For example, "Your cookie is under the chair.", "Your truck is in back of the legos.", "Now stand in front of the line." Begin by using a zero time delay by simultaneously providing the direction and physically assisting the student to follow the direction. Gradually increase the time by 1 second increments. Record a + when the student beats the prompt and complies with the direction. Note, this is **not** an acquisition lesson.

Data Collection

Date	Staff	Activity	Spatial concept	Time delay	Beat the prompt?	Comments

Response Key

Correct: +
Incorrect: -
No response: NR

100												
90												
80												
70												
60												
50												
40												
30												
20												
10												
Date												

Prompt Level Key

FP = full physical
PP = partial physical
M = model
G = gesture
PV = partial verbal
FV = full verbal

Discrete Lesson Plan	Target Skill:	Expressive 'before' and 'after'

Student:	Teacher:	Date:

Behavior objective: Throughout the school day, the student will answer what comes before and/or after in a pre-determined sequence.

Functional association: Domain: School Based   Function: sequencing skills, conceptual skills

Current lesson status [acquisition, fluency, maintenance]: acquisition
(trials/set; # data-points collected per week): 2-3 trials/set, 8 data points/week
Target Criterion (specify type of data: %, frequency, rate, duration, etc.): 90% accuracy, 5 categories, 2 staff

Current **Stimulus Control**: Needs a visual prompt	Long-term **cue**: Before/after question
Discrete Trial format: Yes [maximum # per set] 3 trials/set	Sequential format: No Chained?: No

One vs. Two person prompt?: One	**Prompt Strategy**: Fading (print of visual cues) Pause interval (for hierarchy or delayed):

Error Correction: 4 - step switch

Natural or additional completion R+: praise, earns 5 tokens towards trade in, completion of activity	2nd R+ (during task): tokens, praise: ("You're right! You did pour in the mix after you opened the bag!")
Current 2nd R+ schedule: 1:2 token, praise	Goal 2nd R+ schedule: 1:3 token, 1:2 praise

Generalization (**stimulus factors**): [people, place, materials, supervision, etc.] Vary staff, location, activities, and questions	Generalization (**response factors**): [rate, accuracy, magnitude, duration, etc.] Vary number of trials per set

Parametric details: During functional activities including cooking, arts and crafts, and circle time, display a visual cue showing the sequential order of a target category (e.g. numbers/alphabet letters needed for a game, cooking directions for making a snack etc.). While engaged in an activity such as cooking, ask the student, "What did you do before you opened the bag?" or "What did you do after you got the spoon?" Staff should present the visual cue as a prompt. When the student responds to the question 3 consecutive times correctly, begin to fade the darkness of the symbols displaying the answer. Systematically continue to fade the darkness of the print each time he/she correctly answers the question 3 consecutive times. Work on alphabet and numerical order in the context of a group game. For example, take turns asking the student(s), "What comes before (r)?" or "What comes after (7)?" Students can earn a small token for each correct answer, count them up at the end of the game and the one with the most tokens wins. Implement with speech or PECS students. Indicate + for correct response and - for incorrect responses in the before/after columns.

Data Collection

Date	Staff	Activity	Category	Question	Before	After	Fade	Comments

Response Key

Correct: +
Incorrect: -
No response: NR

100										
90										
80										
70										
60										
50								.		
40										
30										
20										
10										
Date										

Prompt Level Key

FP = full physical
PP = partial physical
M = model
G = gesture
PV = partial verbal
FV = full verbal

Discrete Lesson Plan	Target Skill:	Follow a model

Student:	Teacher:	Date:

Behavior objective: During art, playtime, or cooking, the student will follow a model to complete a simple task.
Functional association: Domain: School Based   Function: imitation, visual discrimination

Current lesson status [acquisition, fluency, maintenance]: acquisition
(trials/set; # data-points collected per week): 10-15 data points per week
Target Criterion (specify type of data: %, frequency, rate, duration, etc.): 3-5 piece assembly,<1 prompt,4 activities, 2 staff

Current **Stimulus Control**: Needs full physical prompting	Long-term **cue**: A completed model

Discrete Trial format: Yes [maximum # per set] 2-3 trials/set	Sequential format: No Chained?: No

One vs. Two person prompt?: **One**	**Prompt Strategy**: Most to Least Prompt Hierarchy - FP, PP, G Pause interval (for hierarchy or delayed):

Error Correction: 4 - step switch

Natural or additional completion R+: praise, earns 5 tokens toward trade in, completes activity	2nd R+ (during task): praise ("Great making it the same!"), earns 5 tokens toward trade in
Current 2nd R+ schedule: 1:1 token, praise	Goal 2nd R+ schedule: 1:2 token, praise

Generalization (**stimulus factors**): [people, place, materials, supervision, etc.] Vary types of activities/materials worked on (e.g., legos, unifix cubes, or pre-cut art activities), vary materials by color, shape, size, and position, vary staff, locations, and vary instruction (e.g., "Do this.", "Make one like mine.")	Generalization (**response factors**): [rate, accuracy, magnitude, duration, etc.] Increase duration of activity, vary number of items used per model, increase complexity of the tasks (e.g., add more pieces) from 2 to 10

Parametric details: Begin by completing things that the child already likes. For example, building a model of blocks = so student can knock them down, building a sequence of beads = so student can wear them, building a chain of trains = so child can play with them. Other preferred items could include, legos, unifix cubes, word/sentence assembly, and pre-cut art. Give the student a completed model and the cue "Make the same." The exact amount of materials should be provided. Start building 3 piece models. Once < 2 prompts per model, add a fourth piece. Once < 2 prompts add 5 piece to sequence until target criteria. Indicate the type of activity worked on, total # of pieces for the activity, and the total # of prompts given for each structure. Begin by fully prompting the student to assemble the model and gradually fade level of prompts. Be sure to pay attention to generalization factors from the start.

Data Collection

Date	Staff	Activity	# of pieces	# of prompts	Comments

Response Key													**Prompt Level Key**
	100												
	90												
	80												
Correct: +	70												FP = full physical
	60												PP = partial physical
Incorrect: -	50												
No response: NR	40												M = model
	30												G = gesture
	20												PV = partial verbal
	10												FV = full verbal
	Date												

Discrete Lesson Plan	Target Skill:	Follow written directions 1

Student:	Teacher:	Date:

Behavior objective: Throughout the school day, the student will read sight words to complete a task.

Functional association: Domain: School Based   Function: reading skills, schedule/direction following

Current lesson status [acquisition, fluency, maintenance]: fluency
(trials/set; # data-points collected per week): 1-3 trials/set, 5-10 data points per week
Target Criterion (specify type of data: %, frequency, rate, duration, etc.): 80% accuracy, 3 staff, 15 words

Current **Stimulus Control**: Needs visual/pictorial prompts	Long-term **cue**: Words involving directions/instructions

Discrete Trial format: Yes *[maximum # per set]* 3 trials/set, disperse 4 sets/week	Sequential format: No Chained?: No

One vs. Two person prompt?: **One**	**Prompt Strategy:** Delayed Prompting (between text and picture) *Pause interval (for hierarchy or delayed):* 1 second progressive time delay (5 sec. Max.)

Error Correction: Backstep interval

Natural or additional completion R+: praise, earns 5 tokens towards trade in, continues/completes activity	2nd R+ (during task): praise ("Great job reading!"), earns 5 tokens towards trade in
Current 2nd R+ schedule: 1:1 praise, 1:1 token	Goal 2nd R+ schedule: 1:2 praise, 1:2 tokens

Generalization (**stimulus factors**): [people, place, materials, supervision, etc.] Vary staff, words, location, activities, and directions given (e.g. "Get the..." or "Go to..."), fade staff proximity	Generalization (**response factors**): [rate, accuracy, magnitude, duration, etc.] Vary amount of trials per set, increase # of steps required

Parametric details: Within activities such as circle time, cooking, art, structured play time, give the student the written sentence "Get the _____." or "Go to (the)_____.", "Put away the _____." completed with a target word. The student will read the word and follow the instruction. Use instructions for which the student can already respond to picture cues and start with 0 second delay and increment by 1 second. Once the student completes the direction, you can label the activity/item. Indicate the time delay or "+" for independent correct responses. There should be NO verbal prompting during the lesson.

Data Collection

Date	Staff	Instructional phrase	Target word	Time delay	Beat the prompt?	Comments

Response Key		**Prompt Level Key**
	100	
	90	
	80	
Correct: +	70	FP = full physical
Incorrect: -	60	PP = partial physical
No response: NR	50	M = model
	40	G = gesture
	30	PV = partial verbal
	20	FV = full verbal
	10	
	Date	

Sequential Lesson Plan	Target Skill:	Follow written directions 2

Student:	Teacher:	Date:

Behavior objective: Throughout the school day, the student will follow written directions.
Functional association: Domain: School Based   Function: reading, domestic skills, direction following

Current lesson status [acquisition, fluency, maintenance]: fluency
(trials/set; # data-points collected per week):5-10 trials/set, 3 data points per week
Target Criterion (specify type of data: %, frequency, rate, duration, etc.): 85% accuracy, 8 activities

Current **Stimulus Control**: Needs gestural to full physical prompting	Long-term **cue**: Written directions

Discrete Trial format: No [maximum # per set] 10 trials/set	Sequential format: Yes Chained?: Yes

One vs. Two person prompt?: **One**	**Prompt Strategy**: Backward chaining Pause interval (for hierarchy or delayed):

Error Correction: Backstep

Natural or additional completion R+: praise, small edible or 2 min. of activity of choice, obtains item	2nd R+ (during task): praise ("Great getting the peanut butter!")
Current 2nd R+ schedule: intermittent praise, small edible or 2 min. of activity of choice upon completion	Goal 2nd R+ schedule: praise at end of task

Generalization (**stimulus factors**): [people, place, materials, supervision, etc.] Vary staff, location (e.g., classroom, home), activities (e.g., packing bags, making brownies, making an art project), fade staff proximity	Generalization (**response factors**): [rate, accuracy, magnitude, duration, etc.] Increase length of lists

Parametric details: The student reads words associated with items within activity. Work on this skill across activities, such as packing bags for outings, gathering supplies for a job, assembling an art project, making cookies, and juice. A list for packing a bag may begin with the direction, "Get the white bag from the closet" and continue with "Get the peanut butter and put it in the bag" until all materials are packed. Each list of directions should have a title that would be written under "Activity." Upon presentation of written direction, guide student to the item. Decrease guidance over trials, using Backstep on errors or pauses longer than 5 seconds. Indicate the level of prompt given for each step of the activity/list being worked on. Vary sequence of directions on lists to avoid memorization of activities.

Data Collection

Date	Prompt	Date	Prompt	Date	Prompt	Comments
Staff		Staff		Staff		
Activity	1.	Activity	1.	Activity	1.	
	2.		2.		2.	
	3.		3.		3.	
	4.		4.		4.	
	5.		5.		5.	
	6.		6.		6.	
	7.		7.		7.	
	8.		8.		8.	
	9.		9.		9.	
	10.		10.		10.	
Total						

Response Key		100											**Prompt Level Key**
		90										
		80										
Correct: +		70										FP = full physical
Incorrect: -		60										PP = partial physical
No response: NR		50										M = model
		40										G = gesture
		30										PV = partial verbal
		20										FV = full verbal
		10										
		Date										

Discrete Lesson Plan	Target Skill:	Follow directions with prepositions

Student:	Teacher:	Date:

Behavior objective: Throughout the day, the student will follow directions involving prepositions.
Functional association: Domain: School Based   Function: independent skills, following directions, prepositions

Current lesson status [acquisition, fluency, maintenance]: fluency
(trials/set; # data-points collected per week): 5 directions a day
Target Criterion (specify type of data: %, frequency, rate, duration, etc.): 85% accuracy, 6 prepositions

Current **Stimulus Control**: Given the direction, (e.g. "Put the basket under the table,") and a gestural prompt to the location	Long-term **cue**: A direction containing a preposition

Discrete Trial format: Yes	Sequential format: No
[maximum # per set] 3 trials/set, dispersed throughout the day	Chained?: No

One vs. Two person prompt?:	**Prompt Strategy**: Delayed Prompting
One	*Pause interval (for hierarchy or delayed):* 1 second progressive time delay (max. 5 sec.)

Error Correction: Built into procedure (decrease next interval upon error)

Natural or additional completion R+: praise paired with token, access to functional/reinforcing item/material	2nd R+ (during task): praise ("Nice putting the cup in the sink."), token
Current 2nd R+ schedule: 1:1 praise, 1:1 token	Goal 2nd R+ schedule: 1:3 praise, 1:4 token

Generalization (**stimulus factors**): [people, place, materials, supervision, etc.] Vary staff, settings (e.g. different classrooms, kitchens, and cafeteria), materials, directions given, fade staff proximity	Generalization (**response factors**): [rate, accuracy, magnitude, duration, etc.] Vary directions relying on contextual cues to ones that do not

Parametric details: Initially, begin with functional/contextual cues and materials. For example, at breakfast, "Put the cup in the sink", and during clean up, "Put the container under the sink." or "Put the blocks in the box.", "Put the chair(s) under the table." Begin by teaching in and under. Start by using a zero time delay by providing the direction and simultaneously prompting the student to complete the direction. Increase the time between providing the direction and the prompt needed to comply by one second increments. Once 80% with these add on. Other examples of functional directions include: before washing hands ("Stand on the stool."), after snack ("Throw in trash.") as well as incorporating directions into the game "Simon Says" (e.g. "Simon says put your hands on your knees.")

Data Collection

Date	Staff	In	Under	On	Behind	In front of	Next to	Time delay	Beat the prompt?	Comments

Response Key

Correct: +
Incorrect: -
No response: NR

100										
90										
80										
70										
60										
50										
40										
30										
20										
10										
Date										

Prompt Level Key

FP = full physical
PP = partial physical
M = model
G = gesture
PV = partial verbal
FV = full verbal

Discrete Lesson Plan	Target Skill:	Label objects by touch

Student:	Teacher:	Date:

Behavior objective: During structured activities, the student will identify objects by touch.

Functional association: Domain: School Based   Function: descriptive skills, expressive language, sensory

Current lesson status [acquisition, fluency, maintenance]: fluency
(trials/set; # data-points collected per week): 5 trials/set, 10 data points per week
Target Criterion (specify type of data: %, frequency, rate, duration, etc.): 30 objects, 90% accuracy

Current **Stimulus Control**: Given the direction, "Tell me what you feel?" and a verbal model of the answer	Long-term **cue**: An object that is not in view
Discrete Trial format: Yes [maximum # per set] 5 trials/set	Sequential format: No Chained?: No

One vs. Two person prompt?: **One**	**Prompt Strategy**: Delayed Prompting to Model *Pause interval (for hierarchy or delayed):* 1 second progressive time delay (max. 5 sec.)

Error Correction: Built into procedure

Natural or additional completion R+: praise, tokens	2nd R+ (during task): praise ("Nice job telling me you touched the orange.") , tokens
Current 2nd R+ schedule: 1:1 token , 1:1 praise	Goal 2nd R+ schedule: 1:4 token, 1:2 praise

Generalization (**stimulus factors**): [people, place, materials, supervision, etc.] Vary staff, materials, items, location (e.g., classroom, cafeteria, home), questions (e.g., "What's in the bag?")	Generalization (**response factors**): [rate, accuracy, magnitude, duration, etc.] Increase the number of items identified/labeled

Parametric details: During structured activities, the student will submerge his/her hand into a bag or into messy media and identify an object in response to the question, "What do you feel?" while immediately modeling the answer. Increase the time delay by 1 second increments every 3rd consecutive correct response. Use objects that the child is somewhat familiar. Consider implementing the "I Spy" game as a means of aiding generalization and including peers.

Data Collection

Date	Staff	Object	Time delay	Beat the prompt?	Comments

Response Key

Correct: +
Incorrect: -
No response: NR

100											
90											
80											
70											
60											
50											
40											
30											
20											
10											
Date											

Prompt Level Key

FP = full physical
PP = partial physical
M = model
G = gesture
PV = partial verbal
FV = full verbal

     Pyramid Educational Consultants

Discrete Lesson Plan	Target Skill:	Answer "Which one is different?"

Student:	Teacher:	Date:

Behavior objective: Throughout the school day, the student will identify objects/pictures that do not belong in a given category by labeling them as different.

Functional association: Domain: School Based   Function: commenting skills, discrimination skills

Current lesson status [acquisition, fluency, maintenance]: acquisition
(trials/set; # data-points collected per week): 3 trials/set, 9 data points per week
Target Criterion (specify type of data: %, frequency, rate, duration, etc.): 80% accuracy across 10 categories, 3 staff

Current **Stimulus Control**: Needs partial physical prompting	Long-term **cue**: Objects/pictures

Discrete Trial format: Yes [maximum # per set] 3 trials/set	Sequential format: No Chained?: No

One vs. Two person prompt?: **One**	Prompt Strategy: Model Pause interval (for hierarchy or delayed):

Error Correction: 4-Step Switch

Natural or additional completion R+: praise, earns 5 tokens towards trade in	2nd R+ (during task): praise ("You're right! The apple is different!"), token
Current 2nd R+ schedule: 1:1 token, praise	Goal 2nd R+ schedule: 1:3 token, 1:2 praise

Generalization (**stimulus factors**): [people, place, materials, supervision, etc.] Vary staff, activities working on, materials, categories, song used/not used	Generalization (**response factors**): [rate, accuracy, magnitude, duration, etc.] Vary number of trials per set, have student tell what makes the others the same and/or why the object is different, vary questions asked (e.g. "Which one is not the same?", "Which one does not belong?")

Parametric details: During group activities such as circle time, snack or arts and crafts, present the student with a group of pictures or objects from a category (e.g. foods, painting materials, animals) and one picture/object that does not belong. Ask the student, "Which one is different?" The student should identify the picture/object that is different. During circle time the lesson can be made into a fun song such as "Which one of these objects doesn't belong?" Note: a prerequisite skill to this lesson is demonstrating grouping objects by category. See **Sorting by category** lesson plan.

Data Collection

Date	Staff	Painting materials	Weather gear	Classroom items	Animals	Foods			Comments

Response Key		**Prompt Level Key**
Correct: + Incorrect: - No response: NR	100 / 90 / 80 / 70 / 60 / 50 / 40 / 30 / 20 / 10 / Date	FP = full physical PP = partial physical M = model G = gesture PV = partial verbal FV = full verbal

Discrete Lesson Plan	**Target Skill:**	**Locate possessions by printed name or photo**	·

Student:	Teacher:	Date:

Behavior objective: Throughout the school day, the student will locate his/her belongings by identifying his/her name and/or picture.
Functional association: Domain: School Based   Function: identify self, name, belongings, independent living skills

Current lesson status [acquisition, fluency, maintenance]: acquisition
(trials/set; # data-points collected per week): 1trial/set, 4 data points per week
Target Criterion (specify type of data: %, frequency, rate, duration, etc.): <1 prompt/5 opportunities, 3 items with name

Current **Stimulus Control**: Needs full physical prompting	Long-term **cue**: Name or picture

Discrete Trial format: Yes [maximum # per set] 1 trial/set	Sequential format: No Chained?: No

One vs. Two person prompt?: **One**	**Prompt Strategy**: Most to Least Prompt Hierarchy - FP, PF, G Pause interval (for hierarchy or delayed):

Error Correction: Provide sufficient prompt level, Backstep if error

Natural or additional completion R+: praise, obtains item, small edible	2nd R+ (during task): praise ("Great getting your bookbag!")
Current 2nd R+ schedule: praise upon getting correct item, 1:1 small edible	Goal 2nd R+ schedule: praise upon independently getting correct item, fade out edible
Generalization (**stimulus factors**): [people, place, materials, supervision, etc.] Vary staff, items located (e.g., locker, turn for line leader, desk), vary location of items, how name is written, pictures of student, fade staff proximity as student locates items more independently	Generalization (**response factors**): [rate, accuracy, magnitude, duration, etc.]

Parametric details: Change location of items on occasion so that the student does not rely on cues other than his/her name and/or picture. For instance, move self care kit to another shelf on the same bookcase or put his/her clipboard on another part of the table. Indicate level of prompt needed to locate each object. Start by teaching the student to locate his/her home/school book. When he/she needs two or less prompts per 5 opportunities, then add teaching the student to locate his/her clipboard. When the student needs two or less prompts per 5 opportunities, add teaching him/her to locate his/her self care kit.

Data Collection

Date	Staff	Home Log	Clipboard	Self care kit	Other:		

Response Key		**Prompt Level Key**
Correct: + Incorrect: - No response: NR	100 / 90 / 80 / 70 / 60 / 50 / 40 / 30 / 20 / 10 / Date	FP = full physical PP = partial physical M = model G = gesture PV = partial verbal FV = full verbal

Discrete Lesson Plan	Target Skill:	Single coin purchase

Student:	Teacher:	Date:

Behavior objective: At scheduled times during the day, the student will use coins.

Functional association: Domain: School Based   Function: money skills, purchasing skills

Current lesson status [acquisition, fluency, maintenance]: fluency
(trials/set; # data-points collected per week): 3-5 trails per set, 10-15 data points per week
Target Criterion (specify type of data: %, frequency, rate, duration, etc.): 90% accuracy, 3 staff, 4 coins (penny, nickel, dime, quarter)

Current **Stimulus Control**: Needs a model	Long-term **cue**: Coins and priced items to buy

Discrete Trial format: Yes [maximum # per set] 5 trials/set	Sequential format: No Chained?: No

One vs. Two person prompt?: **One**	Prompt Strategy: Model Pause interval (for hierarchy or delayed):

Error Correction: 4 -Step Switch

Natural or additional completion R+: natural: gets item (1 minute for toys), praise	2nd R+ (during task): praise ("Nice job giving me the nickel!")
Current 2nd R+ schedule: 1:1natural, praise	Goal 2nd R+ schedule: 1:1natural, 1:2 praise

Generalization (**stimulus factors**): [people, place, materials, supervision, etc.] Vary staff, coins, items for "purchase", cost of item, location, vary cue (e.g., "What would you like?" "What can I get you?")	Generalization (**response factors**): [rate, accuracy, magnitude, duration, etc.] Vary amount of trials per set, have the student take money out of his/her pocket and/or change purse, items should cost under $1.00

Parametric details: Set up a "store" with a variety of objects that the student likes. Label (with a numeric price tag) each item with a price equivalent to a coin amount (e.g., 5 cents), or coin name (e.g., dime). Give the student a variety of coins. To make a "purchase," he/she should hand over the appropriate coin(s). Indicate +/- under the corresponding coin name or amount.

Data Collection

Date	Staff	Penny	Nickel	Dime	Quarter	1 cent	5 cents	10 cents	25 cents	Comments

Response Key

Correct: +
Incorrect: -
No response: NR

100										
90										
80										
70										
60										
50										
40										
30										
20										
10										
Date										

Prompt Level Key

FP = full physical
PP = partial physical
M = model
G = gesture
PV = partial verbal
FV = full verbal

Discrete Lesson Plan	Target Skill:	Gross motor imitation

Student:	Teacher:	Date:

Behavior objective: During games such as "Simon Says" and "The Hokey Pokey", the student will engage in motor imitation.

Functional association: Domain: School Based   Function: imitation, direction following, play skills

Current lesson status [acquisition, fluency, maintenance]: acquisition
(trials/set; # data-points collected per week): 3-5 trials/set, 10-15 data points per week
Target Criterion (specify type of data: %, frequency, rate, duration, etc.): 80% accuracy, 10 actions, 3 staff

Current **Stimulus Control**: Needs full physical prompting	Long-term **cue**: Actions within "Simon Says" and "The Hokey Pokey"
Discrete Trial format: Yes *[maximum # per set]* 5 trials/set, disperse 4 sets across week	Sequential format: No Chained?: No

One vs. Two person prompt? **One**	**Prompt Strategy**: Fading physical prompts (gradually moving physical assistance up the target body part, for example: hand on hand, hand on wrist, hand on forearm, hand on upper arm) Pause interval (for hierarchy or delayed):

Error Correction: Provide sufficient prompt level; increase prompt level on next trial

Natural or additional completion R+: praise, continues/completes game	2nd R+ (during task): praise ("Great job clapping your hands!"), earns 5 tokens towards trade in
Current 2nd R+ schedule: 1:1 praise, 1:1 token	Goal 2nd R+ schedule: 1:2 praise, 1:2 token for independent responses

Generalization (**stimulus factors**): [people, place, materials, supervision, etc.] Vary staff, location, actions imitated, activities working on (e.g., structured playtime), fade staff proximity	Generalization (**response factors**): [rate, accuracy, magnitude, duration, etc.] Vary number of trials per set, increase number of actions modeled per opportunity

Parametric details: During "Simon Says" and the "Hokey Pokey", model the action for the student and use the appropriate games phrase (e.g., "Simon Says, 'Do this', 'Watch me'"). Begin with full physical prompts and gradually fade as needed. Indicate level of prompt given. Write in the action (e.g., clap hands, raise arms, turn around, etc.) you are working on with the student across the top rows of the data collection sheet.

Data Collection

Date	Staff									Comments

Response Key

Correct: +
Incorrect: -
No response: NR

100									
90									
80									
70									
60									
50									
40									
30									
20									
10									
Date									

Prompt Level Key

FP = full physical
PP = partial physical
M = model
G = gesture
PV = partial verbal
FV = full verbal

Discrete Lesson Plan	Target Skill:	Motor imitation with objects

Student:	Teacher:	Date:

Behavior objective: Throughout the day, the student will engage in motor imitation with objects.
Functional association: Domain: School Based   Function: play skills, social skills, imitation

Current lesson status [acquisition, fluency, maintenance]: acquisition
(trials/set; # data-points collected per week): 3-5 trials/set, 10-15 data points per week
Target Criterion (specify type of data: %, frequency, rate, duration, etc.): 80% accuracy, 10 actions

Current **Stimulus Control**: Needs full physical prompting	Long-term **cue**: Objects and modeled action

Discrete Trial format: Yes	Sequential format: No
[maximum # per set] 5 trials/set, disperse 4 sets across week	Chained?: No

One vs. Two person prompt?: **One**	**Prompt Strategy**: Graduated Guidance (hand over hand, hand over wrist, hand on lower arm, hand on elbow, hand on upper arm, hand on shoulder) Pause interval (for hierarchy or delayed):

Error Correction: Use the level of physical assistance needed (increase level on next trial)

Natural or additional completion R+: praise, earns 5 tokens towards trade in, continue/complete activity	2nd R+ (during task): praise ("Very nice wiping the table!"), earns 5 tokens towards trade in
Current 2nd R+ schedule: 1:1 praise, 1:1 token	Goal 2nd R+ schedule: 1:2 praise, token for independent response

Generalization (**stimulus factors**): [people, place, materials, supervision, etc.] Vary staff, work location, items, actions imitated, and activities (e.g., cooking, crafts, structured playtime)	Generalization (**response factors**): [rate, accuracy, magnitude, duration, etc.] Vary number of trials per set, increase number of actions per set

Parametric details: During a variety of activities (e.g., cooking, crafts, and structured playtime), model the action for the student to imitate. Begin by fully prompting the student's response using the prompt strategy outlined above. Gradually fade prompting. Indicate level of prompting needed. In identifying actions for imitation, avoid items for which there is only one action associated because the student will only learn the action based on the object used rather than imitating the action itself. Therefore, when selecting objects for imitation, make sure there are a minimum of two actions associated with each object. Some data collection examples include but are not limited to: (crayon: scribble, tap for dots, color), (ball: bounce, roll, kick, throw), (brush: your hair, dolls hair), (tissue: wipe nose, dab lips), (doll: feed, change clothes, hug, rock to sleep, brush hair), (wet cloth: wipe hands, wipe face, wipe arms) etc.

Data Collection

Date	Staff	Prompt	Object	Action	Prompt	Object	Action	Prompt	Object	Action

Response Key

Correct: +
Incorrect: -
No response: NR

100										
90										
80										
70										
60										
50										
40										
30										
20										
10										
Date										

Prompt Level Key

FP = full physical
PP = partial physical
M = model
G = gesture
PV = partial verbal
FV = full verbal

Discrete Lesson Plan	Target Skill:	Answer questions using media

Student:	Teacher:	Date:

Behavior objective: Given a particular task/situation, the student will use various media resources to obtain information. Functional association: Domain: School Based Function: communication skills, independent work skills, problem solving

Current lesson status [acquisition, fluency, maintenance]: fluency
(trials/set; # data-points collected per week): 1-5 trials/set, 2 data points per week
Target Criterion (specify type of data: %, frequency, rate, duration, etc.): 90% accuracy, 3 staff, 4 resources

Current **Stimulus Control**: Needs verbal prompts	Long-term **cue**: Question requiring media based-information

Discrete Trial format: Yes [maximum # per set] 5 trials/set	Sequential format: No Chained?: No

One vs. Two person prompt?: **One**	**Prompt Strategy**: Delayed prompting (select verbal or gestural) *Pause interval (for hierarchy or delayed):* 1 second progressive time delay (max. 5 sec.)

Error Correction: Decrease next delay interval

Natural or additional completion R+: praise, completes activity	2nd R+ (during task): praise ("Awesome getting the telephone book."), points on point card at completion of activity
Current 2nd R+ schedule: 1:1 praise ("Great finding the phone number!"), points on point card at completion of activity	Goal 2nd R+ schedule: 1:5 praise, points on point card at completion of activity

Generalization (**stimulus factors**): [people, place, materials, supervision, etc.] Vary staff, activities, media resources available and used, questions asked, fade staff proximity	Generalization (**response factors**): [rate, accuracy, magnitude, duration, etc.] Decrease amount of time given to complete the task, increase complexity of question or number of resources needed

Parametric details: This lesson is taught within a variety of activities (e.g., cooking, worksheet(s), circle, and games. The object is for someone to ask the student for information that he/she does not know, but that the student can then obtain by looking in a resource. For example, the student is completing a worksheet requiring specific answers to its questions: definitions of words (dictionary), telephone number (phone book or directory), or during circle time is asked what today's date is (newspaper or calendar). Other examples include, during group work the student is asked the correct spelling of a word (dictionary), what day and time the his/her favorite program is on TV (TV guide), or during cooking the student is given a recipe to cook and needs to know how and what ingredients are needed (cookbook).

Data Collection

Date	Staff	Reason for resource	Resource	# of times used source within activity	Time delay	Beat the prompt (+/-)	Comments

Response Key		**Prompt Level Key**
Correct: + Incorrect: - No response: NR	100 / 90 / 80 / 70 / 60 / 50 / 40 / 30 / 20 / 10 / Date	FP = full physical PP = partial physical M = model G = gesture PV = partial verbal FV = full verbal

Pyramid Educational Consultants

Discrete Lesson Plan	Target Skill:	Raise hand during group activity

Student:	Teacher:	Date:

Behavior objective: When asked a question in a group setting, the student will raise his/her hand to answer.
Functional association: Domain: School Based   Function: communication skills, skill needed for answering questions in a group

Current lesson status [acquisition, fluency, maintenance]: acquisition
(trials/set; # data-points collected per week): 3 trials/set, 3 data points per week
Target Criterion (specify type of data: %, frequency, rate, duration, etc.): 4/5 opportunities independently raising hand, 3 activities

Current **Stimulus Control**: Needs a full physical prompt	Long-term **cue**: When answering a question within a group

Discrete Trial format: Yes [maximum # per set] 3 trial/set	Sequential format: No Chained?: No

One vs. Two person prompt?: **Two**	**Prompt Strategy**: Graduated Guidance (hand over hand, hand over wrist, hand on lower arm, hand on elbow, hand on upper arm) Pause interval (for hierarchy or delayed):

Error Correction: Go back to prompt level needed

Natural or additional completion R+: praise, opportunity to respond, 5 tokens earned toward cash out	2nd R+ (during task): praise, ("Super job raising your hand."), token
Current 2nd R+ schedule:1:1token/raising hand, praise 1:1	Goal 2nd R+ schedule: 1:3 token/raising hand, praise 1:3

Generalization (**stimulus factors**): [people, place, materials, supervision, etc.] Vary staff, activities (e.g., circle, story time, math), locations, number of students in the group, fade staff proximity	Generalization (**response factors**): [rate, accuracy, magnitude, duration, etc.] Vary the number of times staff calls on the student, thin reinforcement schedule of being called upon

Parametric details: During structured activities, such as circle time, show and tell, or storybook time, the student will raise his/her hand to answer questions. Once the communicative partner has asked a question, the physical prompter (standing behind the student) will fully prompt him/her to raise his/her hand. The communicative partner will then call on the student. The physical prompter will systematically fade his/her prompting using the prompts listed above. State the prompt hierarchy level used (FP, PP, +) and location of prompt on arm.

Data Collection

Date	Staff	Activity	Location	Prompt level	Prompt location	Comments

Response Key

Correct: +
Incorrect: -
No response: NR

100												
90												
80												
70												
60												
50												
40												
30												
20												
10												
Date												

Prompt Level Key

FP = full physical
PP = partial physical
M = model
G = gesture
PV = partial verbal
FV = full verbal

Discrete Lesson Plan	Target Skill:	Receptive attributes

Student:	Teacher:	Date:

Behavior objective: Upon being presented with two items and a verbal instruction, the student will select the correct item.
Functional association: Domain: School Based   Function: Follow directions involving attributes

Current lesson status [acquisition, fluency, maintenance]: acquisition
(trials/set; # data-points collected per week): 5 trials/set, 10 data points/week
Target Criterion (specify type of data: %, frequency, rate, duration, etc.): 90% accuracy with 6 attributes

Current **Stimulus Control**: Given direction, (e.g. "Take the big cookie") and a gestural prompt to the item	Long-term **cue**: Items and verbal instruction

Discrete Trial format: Yes [maximum # per set] 5 trials/set	Sequential format: No Chained?: No

One vs. Two person prompt?: **One**	**Prompt Strategy**: Delayed Prompting Pause interval (for hierarchy or delayed):1 second progressive time delay (5 sec max)

Error Correction: Built into procedure; if during delay, block and shorten the next interval

Natural or additional completion R+: natural: after taking the big cup, the student can have juice, praise	2nd R+ (during task): praise ("Excellent job taking the clean towel!"), token
Current 2nd R+ schedule: 1:1 token, 1:1 praise	Goal 2nd R+ schedule: 1:4 token, 1:4 praise

Generalization (**stimulus factors**): [people, place, materials, supervision, etc.] Vary staff, materials (e.g., food, toys, utensils), settings (e.g., cafeteria, classroom, kitchen), activities (e.g., snack, playtime), and staff directions (e.g., "Take the big cup", "Get the little chair")	Generalization (**response factors**): [rate, accuracy, magnitude, duration, etc.]

Parametric details: Work with the student on attributes throughout the day teaching within functional activities. For example, drying hands. After the student washes his/her hands hold out 2 towels (one dirty and one clean) and have him/her take the "clean" one. Begin by working on big and little. Once the student is 70% accurate on these, add dirty and clean. Need to be aware that if teaching one attribute such as "clean" that the polar opposite must also be taught (e.g., "dirty" in a functional context such as laundry: clean towels here and dirty towels there). One must do this for each pair of attributes being taught. Also, understand that initially contextual cues may be used to aid understanding but work towards eliminating them altogether. For example, "take the little ball" because that is the only one that fits the game vs. providing no setting cues at all.

Data Collection

Date	Staff	Big	Little	Dirty	Clean	Length of time delay	Beat the prompt? (+/-)	Comments

Response Key

Correct: +
Incorrect: -
No response: NR

100											
90											
80											
70											
60											
50											
40											
30											
20											
10											
Date											

Prompt Level Key

FP = full physical
PP = partial physical
M = model
G = gesture
PV = partial verbal
FV = full verbal

Pyramid Educational Consultants

Discrete Lesson Plan	Target Skill:	Receptive 'before' and 'after'

Student:	Teacher:	Date:

Behavior objective: In a predetermined sequence (e.g., days of the week, washing hands, going to the bathroom), following a question from the teacher, the student will identify by pointing what comes before and/or after.
Functional association: Domain: School Based   Function: sequencing skills, conceptual skills

Current lesson status [acquisition, fluency, maintenance]: acquisition
(trials/set; # data-points collected per week): 2-3 trials/set, 8 data points per week
Target Criterion (specify type of data: %, frequency, rate, duration, etc.): 80% accuracy, 3 categories, 2 staff

Current **Stimulus Control**: Needs gestural prompting	Long-term **cue**: Before/after events and question

Discrete Trial format: Yes [maximum # per set] 3 trials per set	Sequential format: No Chained?: No

One vs. Two person prompt?: **One**	**Prompt Strategy**: Delayed Prompting *Pause interval (for hierarchy or delayed)*: 1 second progressive time delay (max. 5 sec.)

Error Correction: Block error and decrease next interval

Natural or additional completion R+: praise, earns 5 tokens towards trade in	2nd R+ (during task): praise ("Yes, March does come after February."), tokens
Current 2nd R+ schedule: 1:1 token, praise	Goal 2nd R+ schedule: 1:3 token, 1:2 praise

Generalization (**stimulus factors**): [people, place, materials, supervision, etc.] Vary staff, location, activities, questions asked	Generalization (**response factors**): [rate, accuracy, magnitude, duration, etc.] Vary number of trials per set

Parametric details: During daily activities (e.g., cooking, washing hands, going to the bathroom, swimming, calendar, recess, going home), ask the question what comes before/after while using a visual cue. It is important to establish the routines so that the student is familiar with the sequence and can respond by pointing to the correct answer using the visual cue as a prompt. Therefore, establish the sequence ahead of time. Begin by simultaneously asking the question and gesturing to the correct response. When the student responds three consecutive times correctly, increase the time delay to one second. Continue to gradually increase the time between the target question and providing the gesture to the correct response. When he/she is 80% accurate answering with minimal cues, begin working on another response. Be sure to add additional visuals to the array so the student is discriminating the correct responses. Indicate a + for correct and a - for incorrect response in the before/after columns. If the student beats the prompt then place a line in the time delay column.

Data Collection

Date	Staff	Activity/ sequence	Question	Time delay	**Before**	**After**	Comments

Response Key

Correct: +
Incorrect: -
No response: NR

100											
90											
80											
70											
60											
50											
40											
30											
20											
10											
Date											

Prompt Level Key

FP = full physical
PP = partial physical
M = model
G = gesture
PV = partial verbal
FV = full verbal

Discrete Lesson Plan	**Target Skill:**	**Receptive body part identification**

Student:	Teacher:	Date:

Behavior objective: During activities, such as "Simon Says" and "Follow the Leader", the student will point to or show body parts.
Functional association: Domain: School Based   Function: following directions, body part identification

Current lesson status [acquisition, fluency, maintenance]: acquisition
(trials/set; # data-points collected per week): 5 trials/set, 15 data points/week
Target Criterion (specify type of data: %, frequency, rate, duration, etc.): 80% accurate, 5 body parts

Current **Stimulus Control**: Needs full physical prompting	Long-term **cue**: Cues within Simon Says and Follow the Leader

Discrete Trial format: Yes [maximum # per set] 5 trials/set	Sequential format: No Chained?: No

One vs. Two person prompt?: **One**	**Prompt Strategy**: Fading physical prompts Pause interval (for hierarchy or delayed):

Error Correction: Use level of physical assistance needed

Natural or additional completion R+: completing the game (or access to next activity)	2nd R+ (during task): praise ("Great job touching your head!") 5 tokens earned toward cash out
Current 2nd R+ schedule: 1:1 token, 1:1 praise	Goal 2nd R+ schedule: 1:3 token, 1:2 praise

Generalization (**stimulus factors**): [people, place, materials, supervision, etc.] Vary staff, locations, game played, direction statements given (e.g., "Simon Says, touch your head," "Show me your head."), fade staff proximity	Generalization (**response factors**): [rate, accuracy, magnitude, duration, etc.] Increase the number of body parts learned, have the student take a turn leading the group

Parametric details: During structured activities such as "Simon Says" and "Follow the Leader" have the student follow directions involving identifying body parts. For example, "Simon Says, touch your arm." Staff will begin with a full physical prompt hand over hand to touch the body part and then fade as described above. Begin teaching "head". When the student is 70% independent with identifying "head," add "arm". Add "leg" when the student is 70% independent with "arm". When providing prompts, regulate the level of intensity of physical assistance. Indicate the level of prompt given. Record a + when the student independently identifies the appropriate body part.

Data Collection

Date	Staff	Game	Head	Arm	Leg	Eyes	Mouth	Comments

Response Key	100										**Prompt Level Key**
	90										
	80										
Correct: +	70										FP = full physical
	60										PP = partial physical
Incorrect: -	50										M = model
No response: NR	40										G = gesture
	30										PV = partial verbal
	20										FV = full verbal
	10										
	Date										

Pyramid Educational Consultants

Discrete Lesson Plan	Target Skill:	Receptive color identification

Student:	Teacher:	Date:

Behavior objective: Given a colored item and a verbal instruction, the student will select according to color.
Functional association: Domain: School Based   Function: follow directions involving colors

Current lesson status [acquisition, fluency, maintenance]: acquisition
(trials/set; # data-points collected per week): 6 trials/set, 12 data points per week
Target Criterion (specify type of data : %, frequency, rate, duration, etc.): 80% accuracy across 3 days, 2 staff

Current **Stimulus Control**: Being asked, "Give me ___", with a gestural prompt to the item	Long-term **cue**: Colored items and instruction

Discrete Trial format: Yes [maximum # per set] 5 trials/set	Sequential format: No Chained?: No

One vs. Two person prompt?: **One**	**Prompt Strategy**: Delayed Prompting (from verbal cue to gestural) Pause interval (for hierarchy or delayed): 3 seconds (fixed)

Error Correction: Block error and decrease next interval

Natural or additional completion R+: natural: (e.g., "Do you want juice? Give me "red" cup."… gets juice in cup)	2nd R+ (during task): praise ("Nice giving me the "red" cup.")
Current 2nd R+ schedule: 1:1	Goal 2nd R+ schedule: 1:4

Generalization (**stimulus factors**): [people, place, materials, supervision, etc.] Vary staff, settings, activities, materials (e.g., need cups, toys, paper), vary verbal directions given (e.g., "Give me ____." , "Take the ___crayon."), vary colors of items	Generalization (**response factors**): [rate, accuracy, magnitude, duration, etc.] Increase direction complexity (e.g., "Get me a red ball and a blue crayon.")

Parametric details: Throughout the school day, work with the student on colors using functional activities and items.(different colored bubble containers, legos, paints, crayons, candy, etc). Note that the color of the object must already be important to the student. If the child does not indicate a color preference (e.g., always takes red Popsicle, uses purple crayons/markers, builds with blue legos), then begin by placing a preferred toy or snack item in a red bag paired with a different colored container and see if the child retrieves the item by saying, "It's in the red bag." Note, initially the student watches you hide the item. Continue this procedure varying items hidden and the color of the containers. Target red and yellow first. After 80% accurate on these add an additional color. This method of teaching provides a functional contextual basis for the lesson because it makes the attribute (color) important to the child because it contains their preferred item. Once color is established, move to more arbitrary phrases such as, "Take the ____ (item)." and "Give me ___."

Data Collection

Date	Staff	Red	Yellow	Blue	Green	Orange	Purple	Pink	Brown	Black	White	Comments

Response Key

Correct: +
Incorrect: -
No response: NR

100									
90									
80									
70									
60									
50									
40									
30									
20									
10									
Date									

Prompt Level Key

FP = full physical
PP = partial physical
M = model
G = gesture
PV = partial verbal
FV = full verbal

Discrete Lesson Plan	Target Skill:	Receptive object counting

Student:	Teacher:	Date:

Behavior objective: Throughout the day, the student will count out a predetermined number of items.

Functional association: Domain: School Based   Function: math skills, direction following

Current lesson status [acquisition, fluency, maintenance]: acquisition
(trials/set; # data-points collected per week): 3-5 trials/set, 5-10 data points per week
Target Criterion (specify type of data: %, frequency, rate, duration, etc.): 80% accuracy, 3 staff, numbers 1-5

Current **Stimulus Control**: Needs a full physical prompt	Long-term **cue**: Items and a specific request

Discrete Trial format: Yes	Sequential format: No
[maximum # per set] 5 trials/set, disperse 4 sets across week	Chained?: No

One vs. Two person prompt?:	**Prompt Strategy**: Fading physical prompts
One	Pause interval (for hierarchy or delayed): 3 seconds

Error Correction: Provide sufficient prompt level; increase level on next trial

Natural or additional completion R+: praise, continues/completes activity	2nd R+ (during task): praise ("Nice getting 3 spoons for breakfast."), earns 5 tokens towards trade in
Current 2nd R+ schedule: 1:1 praise, 1:1 token	Goal 2nd R+ schedule: 1:2 praise, 1:2 tokens

Generalization (**stimulus factors**): [people, place, materials, supervision, etc.] Vary staff, location, activity (e.g., cooking and art), number working on, cue given (e.g., "Get 3 ____." "Give me 4 ____." "Get 2 ____.", and items gathered	Generalization (**response factors**): [rate, accuracy, magnitude, duration, etc.] Vary amount of trials per set, decrease time spent counting, maximum 10 items

Parametric details: Teach within functional/relevant contexts from the student's perspective. For example, the student needs 3 more pieces to complete a puzzle, 5 colors to complete an art project, 2 shoes/boots to dress the weather bear, and needs 1 coin for connect four. It is important that the desired items, not the desired number, be laid out for the student to obtain. Remember this is a receptive task and counting the objects is not the objective. Teach within activities such as circle time, cooking, art, and structured playtime. Give the student the direction, "Get 3 _____." Indicate the level of prompt given or "+" for independent correct response for each number.

Data Collection

Date	Staff	1	2	3	4	5			Comments

Response Key		**Prompt Level Key**
Correct: + Incorrect: - No response: NR	100 90 80 70 60 50 40 30 20 10 Date	FP = full physical PP = partial physical M = model G = gesture PV = partial verbal FV = full verbal

Pyramid Educational Consultants

Discrete Lesson Plan	Target Skill:	Receptive sight words

Student:	Teacher:	Date:

Behavior objective: Throughout the school day, the student will read sight words to complete a task.

Functional association: Domain: School Based   Function: reading skills, schedule/direction following

Current lesson status [acquisition, fluency, maintenance]: fluency
(trials/set; # data-points collected per week):1-3 trials set, 5-10 data points per week
Target Criterion (specify type of data: %, frequency, rate, duration, etc.): 80% accuracy, 3 staff, 15 words

Current **Stimulus Control**: Needs a full physical prompt	Long-term **cue**: Words

Discrete Trial format: Yes *[maximum # per set]* 3 trials/set, disperse 4 sets across week	Sequential format: No Chained?: No

One vs. Two person prompt?: **One**	**Prompt Strategy**: Most to least Prompt Hierarchy - FP, PP, G Pause interval (for hierarchy or delayed): 3 seconds

Error Correction: 4-step switch

Natural or additional completion R+: praise, earns 5 tokens towards trade in, access to cued activity	2nd R+ (during task): praise ("Great job reading!"), earns 5 tokens towards trade in
Current 2nd R+ schedule: 1:1 praise, 1:1 token	Goal 2nd R+ schedule: 1:2 praise, 1:2 tokens

Generalization (**stimulus factors**): [people, place, materials, supervision, etc.] Vary staff, words, location, activity working on, direction given (e.g., "Get the ___." or "Go to ___.")	Generalization (**response factors**): [rate, accuracy, magnitude, duration, etc.] Vary number of trials per set

Parametric details: Within activities such as circle time, cooking, art, and structured play time, give the student the written sentence "Get the _____" or "Go to (the)_____" completed with a sight word. He/she should either get the appropriate item or go to that activity/area. Start with functional directions, for example: going to the door leads to going outside, going to the refrigerator leads to getting a snack/drink. Over time staff can add a game-like quality: run to the door, touch the floor, and sit down. Begin teaching with a full physical prompt and fade prompt intensity to a partial physical and then a gesture as the student becomes more independent with each word. Indicate the level of prompt given or "+" for independent correct responses and not direction format for each word ("Get" or "Go to").

Data Collection

Date	Staff	Word	Word	Word	Word	Get:	Go to:	Comments
						☐	☐	
						☐	☐	
						☐	☐	
						☐	☐	
						☐	☐	
						☐	☐	
						☐	☐	
						☐	☐	
						☐	☐	
						☐	☐	
						☐	☐	

Response Key

Correct: +
Incorrect: -
No response: NR

100										
90										
80										
70										
60										
50										
40										
30										
20										
10										
Date										

Prompt Level Key

FP = full physical
PP = partial physical
M = model
G = gesture
PV = partial verbal
FV = full verbal

Discrete Lesson Plan	Target Skill:	Expressive sight words	·

Student:	Teacher:	Date:

Behavior objective: During structured and unstructured activities, the student will read sight words.
Functional association: Domain: School Based   Function: reading skills, schedule/direction following

Current lesson status [acquisition, fluency, maintenance]: acquisition
(trials/set; # data-points collected per week): 5-10 trials/set, 15 data points per week
Target Criterion (specify type of data: %, frequency, rate, duration, etc.): 80% accuracy, 3 staff, 10 words

Current **Stimulus Control**: Needs a model	Long-term **cue**: Words
Discrete Trial format: Yes [maximum # per set] 3 trials/activity	Sequential format: No Chained?: No

One vs. Two person prompt?: **One**	**Prompt Strategy**: Delayed Prompting *Pause interval (for hierarchy or delayed):* 1 second progressive time delay (max. 5 sec.)

Error Correction: Built into procedure

Natural or additional completion R+: praise, earns 5 tokens towards trade in, obtains item	2nd R+ (during task): praise ("Great job reading!"), token
Current 2nd R+ schedule: 1:1 praise, 1:1 token	Goal 2nd R+ schedule: 1:3 praise, 1:3 tokens
Generalization (**stimulus factors**): [people, place, materials, supervision, etc.] Vary staff, words, location, vary form of request (e.g., "What does it say?" or "Read this, please."), vary presentation of words (e.g., different order)	Generalization (**response factors**): [rate, accuracy, magnitude, duration, etc.] Vary amount of trials per set, have student follow simple directions by reading the words, have student read the word and then take the corresponding item or go to that activity

Parametric details: During activities, such as making pudding, painting, arts and crafts, and breakfast, incorporate sight words into items needed for the task. For example, while making pudding, the student will need a spoon to stir the mixture. Hold up the word spoon and simultaneously point to the spoon. Continue to increase by 1-second intervals as student indicates successful trials. Use the same technique applied to needed arts and crafts materials, holding up the word while gesturing to the item. Note: if an item is held up, student can already name it out loud, he/she does not require a model from staff. Therefore, you are switching stimulus control from naming the object to reading the name of the object.

Data Collection

Date	Staff	Word	Length of time delay	Beat the prompt?	Comments

Response Key		**Prompt Level Key**

	100										
	90										
	80										
	70										
	60										
	50										
	40										
	30										
	20										
	10										
	Date										

Response Key

Correct: +
Incorrect: -
No response: NR

Prompt Level Key

FP = full physical
PP = partial physical
M = model
G = gesture
PV = partial verbal
FV = full verbal

Pyramid Educational Consultants

Discrete Lesson Plan	Target Skill:	Sort silverware

Student:	Teacher:	Date:

Behavior objective: During scheduled times or when emptying the dishwasher, the student will sort silverware into a silverware holder.

Functional association: Domain: School Based   Function: independent work/living skills, visual discrimination skills

Current lesson status [acquisition, fluency, maintenance]: acquisition
(trials/set; # data-points collected per week): 2 data points per week
Target Criterion (specify type of data: %, frequency, rate, duration, etc.): 85% accuracy, across 2 staff

Current **Stimulus Control**: Needs gestures to full physical prompts and one example per category as a model	Long-term **cue**: Clean silverware in dishwasher

Discrete Trial format: Yes [maximum # per set] 1 trial/set	Sequential format: No Chained?: No

One vs. Two person prompt?: **One**	**Prompt Strategy**: Delayed Prompting *Pause interval (for hierarchy or delayed)*:1 second progressive time delay (max. 5 sec.)

Error Correction: Built into procedure

Natural or additional completion R+: praise, cashes out 5 tokens for small edible or activity of choice (cash out should coincide with completion of sorting)	2nd R+ (during task): verbal praise ("Nice sorting the silverware, _____."), tokens
Current 2nd R+ schedule: intermittent praise, earns 1 token VI- 3 min for appropriate working	Goal 2nd R+ schedule: praise & earns 1 token VI- 5 min. for appropriate working
Generalization (**stimulus factors**): [people, place, materials, supervision, etc.] Vary staff, work location and types of silverware (e.g., plastic, metal and colored), fade staff proximity	Generalization (**response factors**): [rate, accuracy, magnitude, duration, etc.] Decrease the time it takes to complete the task

Parametric details: Initially, as the student picks up the utensil, simultaneously gesture to the correct slot for that piece of silverware. As the students ability increases to correctly sort the silverware, increase the delay by one second intervals.

Data Collection

Date	Staff	Spoon	Knife	Fork	Delay length	Comments

Response Key

Correct: +
Incorrect: -
No response: NR

100												
90												
80			·									
70												
60												
50												
40												
30												
20												
10												
Date												

Prompt Level Key

FP = full physical
PP = partial physical
M = model
G = gesture
PV = partial verbal
FV = full verbal

Discrete Lesson Plan	Target Skill:	Sort by category

Student:	Teacher:	Date:

Behavior objective: When cleaning up after playtime, the student will correctly put away toys by sorting them.
Functional association: Domain: School Based   Function: categorization skills

Current lesson status [acquisition, fluency, maintenance]: fluency
(trials/set; # data-points collected per week): 1 trial/set, 3 data points per week
Target Criterion (specify type of data: %, frequency, rate, duration, etc.): 80% accurate across 10 sets of objects

Current **Stimulus Control**: Needs gestural prompting	Long-term **cue**: Out-of-place toys

Discrete Trial format: Yes [maximum # per set] 25 trials/set	Sequential format: No Chained?: No

One vs. Two person prompt?: **One**	**Prompt Strategy**: Delayed Prompting *Pause interval (for hierarchy or delayed)*: 1 second progressive time delay (max. 5 sec.)

Error Correction: Built into procedure

Natural or additional completion R+: praise, tokens, access to next activity	2nd R+ (during task): praise ("Great sorting the cars!"), tokens
Current 2nd R+ schedule: intermittent praise, 1 token to 5 objects, cash out at 5 tokens	Goal 2nd R+ schedule: praise at completion of task(s), 1 token to 15 objects, cash out at 5 tokens

Generalization (**stimulus factors**): [people, place, materials, supervision, etc.] Vary staff, materials, locations (e.g., gym, classroom, playground)	Generalization (**response factors**): [rate, accuracy, magnitude, duration, etc.] Vary number of materials, increase rate at which the student sorts the objects

Parametric details: During clean-up from playtime, domestic play, or other functional activities, the student will sort the objects into their correct location. Record the number of objects he/she had to sort and the correct number he/she sorted. Examples of categories may include but are not limited to: blocks vs. balls, cars vs. books, napkins vs. plates, legos vs. beads, and markers vs. crayons. Note: the student should be able to sort two-way, three-way, four-way etc. Do not limit student to just sorting two different objects. Gradually increase number of different objects that need sorting.

Data Collection

Date	Staff	Objects	# to sort	# correctly sorted	Time delay	Beat the prompt?	Comments

Response Key												**Prompt Level Key**
	100											
	90											
	80											
Correct: +	70											FP = full physical
	60											PP = partial physical
Incorrect: -	50											M = model
No response: NR	40											
	30											G = gesture
	20											PV = partial verbal
	10											FV = full verbal
	Date											

Sequential Lesson Plan	Target Skill:	Walk in hallway

Student:	Teacher:	Date:

Behavior objective: During transitions outside the classroom, the student will walk in the hallway.

Functional association: Domain: School Based   Function: independent skills for the community

Current lesson status [acquisition, fluency, maintenance]: acquisition
(trials/set; # data-points collected per week) 1 trial/set, 2 data points per week
Target Criterion (specify type of data: %, frequency, rate, duration, etc.): < 2 prompts, 10 minutes, 3 locations, 3 staff

Current **Stimulus Control**: Staff shadow student	Long-term **cue**: Hallway

Discrete Trial format: No [maximum # per set] 1	Sequential format: Yes Chained?: No

One vs. Two person prompt?: **One**	**Prompt Strategy**: Shaping (reinforcement) and Fading (proximity) Pause interval (for hierarchy or delayed):

Error Correction: Backstep

Natural or additional completion R+: praise, small edible, gets to target area	2nd R+ (during task): praise ("Nice walking.")
Current 2nd R+ schedule: praise, edible every 6 seconds	Goal 2nd R+ schedule: praise, edible every 1 minute

Generalization (**stimulus factors**): [people, place, materials, supervision, etc.] Vary staff, location (e.g., different hallways), fade staff proximity	Generalization (**response factors**): [rate, accuracy, magnitude, duration, etc.] Increase the length of hallways, thin rate of reinforcement

Parametric details: The goal is for the student to walk in the hallway without prompting. Staff begin by shadowing the student by placing one hand behind him/her (casually) while walking. Give R+ every 6 seconds for nice walking and again at reaching destination. After 5 successful trials of no shadowing move one foot away from student. Reinforce the walking at that distance if he/she has not darted during that six-second period. Continue to increase distance after 5 successful trials. Only reinforce if the student has not run during that interval at the present distance. Gradually increase the interval.

Data Collection

Date	Staff	Destination	Shadowing?		# of feet	# seconds receive R+	# R+ given	Comments
			Yes	No				

Response Key

Correct: +
Incorrect: -
No response: NR

100											
90											
80											
70											
60											
50											
40											
30											
20											
10											
Date											

Prompt Level Key

FP = full physical
PP = partial physical
M = model
G = gesture
PV = partial verbal
FV = full verbal

Self-Help Lesson Plans

Sequential Lesson Plan	Target Skill:	Brush hair

Student:	Teacher:	Date:

Behavior objective: At specified times during the school day, the student will brush his/her hair.

Functional association: Domain: Self Help   Function: independent living skills, hygiene

Current lesson status [acquisition, fluency, maintenance]: acquisition
(trials/set; # data-points collected per week):1 trial/set, 2 data points per week
Target Criterion (specify type of data: %, frequency, rate, duration, etc.): 80% accurate, 3 staff, 2 brushes

Current **Stimulus Control**: Needs full physical prompting	Long-term **cue**: Picture of "brush hair" on schedule
Discrete Trial format: No [maximum # per set]	Sequential format: Yes Chained?: Forward Chain

One vs. Two person prompt?: **One**	Prompt Strategy: Fading Pause interval (for hierarchy or delayed):

Error Correction: Use level of physical assistance needed

Natural or additional completion R+: praise and edible	2nd R+ (during task): praise (" Nice brushing your hair.")
Current 2nd R+ schedule: 1:1 edible, 1:1 praise	Goal 2nd R+ schedule: praise and edible given at end of task

Generalization (**stimulus factors**): [people, place, materials, supervision, etc.] vary staff, brushes, location (e.g., school bathroom, group home bathroom, home bathroom), time of day, decrease proximity	Generalization (**response factors**): [rate, accuracy, magnitude, duration, etc.] Reduce time it takes the student to brush their hair

Parametric details: Fully prompt the student to touch the brush to his/her head. Once he/she does this for 3 independent trials increase to touching brush to head and making 1 stroke with the brush from the top of their head to the end of their hair. Once he/she has 3 independent trials on this step, add the next step to the sequence. Always begin by fully prompting and reinforcing the first trial of the new step. Then only reinforce the independent steps. Note: verbal and partial verbal prompts are not options in the 'prompt level key'.

Task Analysis Data Collection

Steps:	Date:											
1. Pick up brush												
2. Stroke hair with brush from top of head to end of hair (side 1)												
3. Repeat												
4. Stroke hair with brush from top of head to end of hair (side 2)												
5. Repeat"												
6. Stroke hair with brush from top of head to end of hair (back)												
7. Repeat												
Total:												
Staff:												

Response Key

Correct: +
Incorrect: -
No response: NR

100													
90													
80													
70													
60													
50													
40													
30													
20													
10													
Date													

Prompt Level Key

FP = full physical
PP = partial physical
M = model
G = gesture
PV = partial verbal
FV = full verbal

Sequential Lesson Plan	Target Skill:	Brush teeth

Student:	Teacher:	Date:

Behavior objective: At scheduled times, such as after breakfast or lunch, the student will brush his/her teeth.
Functional association: Domain: Self Help   Function: independent living skills, hygiene

Current lesson status [acquisition, fluency, maintenance]: acquisition
(trials/set; # data-points collected per week): 3 data points per week
Target Criterion (specify type of data: %, frequency, rate, duration, etc.): 80% accuracy across 2 staff

Current **Stimulus Control**: Needs full physical prompting	Long-term **cue**: Obtain schedule card following meal clean-up
Discrete Trial format: No [maximum # per set]	Sequential format: Yes Chained?: Backward Chain

One vs. Two person prompt?: **One**	**Prompt Strategy**: Fading prompt level at target step Pause interval (for hierarchy or delayed):

Error Correction: Backstep if not on target step

Natural or additional completion R+: praise, 2 minutes of chosen activity	2nd R+ (during task): praise ("Nice rinsing the brush.")
Current 2nd R+ schedule: intermittent praise	Goal 2nd R+ schedule: praise at completion of task

Generalization (**stimulus factors**): [people, place, materials, supervision, etc.] Vary staff, location, materials (e.g., types of toothpaste, toothbrushes), fade staff once student is able to complete all steps independently	Generalization (**response factors**): [rate, accuracy, magnitude, duration, etc.] Increase time to 2 minute maximum

Parametric details: Materials are located on shelf in bathroom. Staff should complete all steps of the task analysis except the target step. Teach the target step by fading from full physical prompts. Once 80% accurate on target step, add prior step to the sequence, allowing student to complete the remainder of the step(s) independently. Note: partial verbal and verbal prompts are not options in the 'prompt level key'.

Task Analysis   :

1. Get materials	8. Put paste on brush	15. Obtain cup
2. Take to sink	9. Put cap on	16. Fill with water
3. Pick up toothbrush	10. Put paste away	17. Rinse mouth
4. Turn water on	11. Put brush in mouth	18. Put cup away
5. Wet brush	12. Brush entire mouth	19. Get towel
6. Get toothpaste	13. Rinse brush	20. Dry mouth
7. Take cap off	14. Put brush away	21. Throw towel away

Target Step	Date													
Total:														
Staff:														

Response Key

Correct: +
Incorrect: -
No response: NR

100												
90												
80												
70												
60												
50												
40												
30												
20												
10												
Date												

Prompt Level Key

FP = full physical
PP = partial physical
M = model
G = gesture
PV = partial verbal
FV = full verbal

Sequential Lesson Plan	Target Skill:	Button

Student:	Teacher:	Date:

Behavior objective: At naturally occurring opportunities (e.g., dressing, putting on a smock), the student will fasten buttons on his/her clothes.

Functional association: Domain: Self Help   Function: independent living skills, dressing

Current lesson status [acquisition, fluency, maintenance]: acquisition
(trials/set; # data-points collected per week):3 data points per week
Target Criterion (specify type of data: %, frequency, rate, duration, etc.): 85% accuracy with large and small buttons, 3 staff

Current **Stimulus Control**: Needs full physical prompting	Long-term **cue**: Unbuttoned button on his/her clothes
Discrete Trial format: No [maximum # per set]	Sequential format: Yes Chained?: Backward Chain

One vs. Two person prompt?: **One**	**Prompt Strategy**: Fade prompts at target step Pause interval (for hierarchy or delayed):

Error Correction: Backstep if not on target step

Natural or additional completion R+: praise, earns tokens for buttoning, cash out when has 5 tokens, access to next activity	2nd R+ (during task): praise ("Great buttoning your buttons!"), earns tokens
Current 2nd R+ schedule: 1:1 praise, 1:2 tokens (1 token for every 2 buttons fastened)	Goal 2nd R+ schedule: 1:3 praise (praise for every 3 buttons fastened), 1:5 tokens (1 token for every 5 buttons fastened)

Generalization (**stimulus factors**): [people, place, materials, supervision, etc.] Vary staff, locations, articles of clothing (e.g., coats, pants, shirts) and size of buttons, fade staff proximity for independent steps	Generalization (**response factors**): [rate, accuracy, magnitude, duration, etc.] Increase and vary the number of buttons to be fastened

Parametric details: Fully prompt through all steps until the last step. Teach this step using the needed prompt (no verbal prompts). Indicate the level of prompt necessary. Once the student is 80% accurate with this step, add prior step, allowing the student to complete the remainder of steps independently. Work on this skill when changing into and out of gym clothes, putting on smocks for messy activities, putting on coat to go outside or to leave for the day.

Task Analysis
1. Hold material close to button hole between thumb and forefinger
2. Hold button with other hand
3. Pull material open at button hole
4. Slide one side of button into hole
5. Push whole button through hole

Target Step	Date												
Total:													
Staff:													

Response Key

Correct: +
Incorrect: -
No response: NR

100										
90										
80										
70										
60										
50										
40										
30										
20										
10										
Date										

Prompt Level Key

FP = full physical
PP = partial physical
M = model
G = gesture
PV = partial verbal
FV = full verbal

Sequential Lesson Plan	Target Skill:	Comb hair

Student:	Teacher:	Date:

Behavior objective: After activities such as gym and recess, the student will comb his/her hair.
Functional association: Domain: Self Help   Function: independent living skills, hygiene

Current lesson status [acquisition, fluency, maintenance]: acquisition
(trials/set; # data-points collected per week): 3 data points per week
Target Criterion (specify type of data: %, frequency, rate, duration, etc.): 80% accuracy, 3 staff

Current **Stimulus Control**: Needs full physical prompting	Long-term **cue**: "Comb hair" on picture schedule

Discrete Trial format: No [maximum # per set]	Sequential format: Yes Chained?: Forward Chain

One vs. Two person prompt?: **One**	Prompt Strategy: Fading Pause interval (for hierarchy or delayed):

Error Correction: Use level of physical assistance needed

Natural or additional completion R+: praise, small edible upon completion of task, access to next activity	2nd R+ (during task): praise ("Nice job combing your hair!")
Current 2nd R+ schedule: small edible upon completion of task, intermittent praise	Goal 2nd R+ schedule: praise upon completion of task

Generalization (**stimulus factors**): [people, place, materials, supervision, etc.] Vary staff, time of day, type of comb, location, and fade staff proximity	Generalization (**response factors**): [rate, accuracy, magnitude, duration, etc.] Decrease time it takes student to complete task

Parametric details: After activities such as gym and recess, the student will comb his/her hair. Teach the first step using the prompt strategy and then fully prompt through the rest of the task. After 3 independent responses on the first step, add the second step to the sequence allowing the student to complete the first step independently. Continue to fully prompt through the rest of the task analysis adding steps to the sequence after 3 independent responses of the target step. Mark + for independent responses and the level of prompting needed for the other steps.

Task Analysis

Steps Date:												
1. Go to mirror												
2. Pick up comb												
3. Lift comb to top of right side of head												
4. Pull comb down through hair to bottom												
5. Lift comb to top of back of head												
6. Pull comb down through hair to bottom												
7. Lift comb to top of left side of head												
8. Pull comb down through hair to bottom												
9. Lift comb to top of front of head												
10. Pull comb down through hair to bottom												
11. Look in mirror to check hair												
12. Re-comb missed areas												
Total												
Staff												

Response key	100											**Prompt level key**
	90											FP = full physical
	80						.					PP = partial physical
	70											M = model
Correct: +	60											G = gesture
	50											
Incorrect: −	40											PV = partial verbal
	30											FV = full verbal
No response: **NR**	20											
	10											
	date											

Sequential Lesson Plan	Target Skill:	Dressing

Student:	Teacher:	Date:

Behavior objective: Before and after gym or recess, the student will get dressed.
Functional association: Domain: Self Help   Function: independent living skills

Current lesson status [acquisition, fluency, maintenance]: acquisition
(trials/set; # data-points collected per week): 2 data points per week
Target Criterion (specify type of data: %, frequency, rate, duration, etc.): 70% of TA across 3 trials

Current **Stimulus Control**: Needs physical prompting	Long-term **cue**: "Change" as indicated on picture schedule

Discrete Trial format: No [maximum # per set]	Sequential format: Yes Chained?: Backward Chain

One vs. Two person prompt?: **One**	**Prompt Strategy**: Fade prompt at target step Pause interval (for hierarchy or delayed)

Error Correction: Backstep if not on target step

Natural or additional completion R+: natural: goes to gym or recess, praise	2nd R+ (during task): praise (" Terrific putting on your shirt.")
Current 2nd R+ schedule: praise for each step	Goal 2nd R+ schedule: praise at completion of task

Generalization (**stimulus factors**): [people, place, materials, supervision, etc.] Vary staff, location (e.g., bathroom, classroom, locker room,), clothes (e.g., shorts, pants), and fade staff proximity as student increases independence	Generalization (**response factors**): [rate, accuracy, magnitude, duration, etc.] Decrease time needed to complete task

Parametric details: Given "change" on schedule, the student will get his/her basket from the shelf. Once seated and undressed (see "Undress" lesson plan), staff will fully prompt (no verbal prompts) student through all steps until the target step. At this step, teach using necessary prompt level. Once the student has reached 3 independent responses on the last step, then add the second to last step to the sequence. The student will then complete the remaining step(s) independently.

Task Analysis Data Collection

Steps: Shirt/Pants Date"														
1. Picks up shirt from bottom with both hands														
2. Puts shirt over her head														
3. Pull head through														
4. Puts arm # 1 in the sleeve														
5. Puts arm #2 in the other sleeve														
6. Pulls shirt down to waist														
1. Pick up pants at waist														
2. Put leg #1 in one pant leg														
3. Put leg #2 in the other pant leg														
4. Pull feet through														
5. Stand up														
6. Pull pants to waist														
Total:														
Staff:														

Response Key	100											**Prompt Level Key**
	90											
	80											
Correct: +	70											FP = full physical
Incorrect: -	60											PP = partial physical
No response: NR	50											M = model
	40											G = gesture
	30											PV = partial verbal
	20											FV = full verbal
	10											
	Date											

Sequential Lesson Plan	Target Skill:	Wash hands

Student:	Teacher:	Date:

Behavior objective: After using the toilet, messy activities, eating, and before cooking, the student will wash hands.
Functional association: Domain: Self Help   Function: independent living skills, safety, hygiene

Current lesson status [acquisition, fluency, maintenance]: acquisition
(trials/set; # data-points collected per week): 3 data points per week
Target Criterion (specify type of data: %, frequency, rate, duration, etc.): 85% accuracy, across 2 staff, 3 different sinks

Current **Stimulus Control**: Needs full physical prompting	Long-term **cue**: Finishing toileting sequence, having dirty hands, before eating or cooking
Discrete Trial format: No [maximum # per set]	Sequential format: Yes Chained?: Backward Chain
One vs. Two person prompt? **One**	**Prompt Strategy**: Prompt Hierarchy - Fade physical prompt at target step Pause interval (for hierarchy or delayed):

Error Correction: Backstep if not on target step

Natural or additional completion R+: small edible, praise, access next activity	2nd R+ (during task): praise: ("Great job getting the soap.")
Current 2nd R+ schedule: intermittent praise, small edible upon completion of sequence	Goal 2nd R+ schedule: praise at task completion (fade out edible)
Generalization (**stimulus factors**): [people, place, materials, etc.] Vary staff, vary location (e.g., different bathrooms, sinks), vary types of soap and towels used, fade staff proximity for independent steps	Generalization (**response factors**): [rate, accuracy, magnitude, duration, etc.] Decrease amount of time given to complete the task

Parametric details: Fully prompt the student through all steps until the last step. Teach this step using the prompt hierarchy (avoiding all verbal prompts). Indicate level of prompt needed. Once the student meets criteria for the target step, add the prior step to the sequence. Teach this by fading physical and gestural prompts. Allow the student to complete the remainder of the step(s) independently.

Task Analysis Data Collection

1. Turn on water	5. Push soap	9. Orient towards towel
2. Wet one hand	6. Rub hands together	10. Get towel
3. Wet second hand	7. Rinse hands	11. Dry hands
4. Place hand under soap	8. Turn off water	

Target Step	Date													
Total:														
Staff:														

Response Key

Correct: +
Incorrect: -
No response: NR

100													
90													
80													
70													
60													
50													
40													
30													
20													
10													
Date													

Prompt Level Key

FP = full physical
PP = partial physical
M = model
G = gesture
PV = partial verbal
FV = full verbal

Sequential Lesson Plan	Target Skill:	Pour liquid into glass

Student:	Teacher:	Date:

Behavior objective: In a situation that requires the student to get himself/herself or someone else something to drink, he/she will pour the liquid from a container into a glass.
Functional association: Domain: Self Help   Function: independent living, fine motor skills, eye-hand coordination

Current lesson status [acquisition, fluency, maintenance]: acquisition
(trials/set; # data-points collected per week):1-2 trials/set, 4 data points per week
Target Criterion (specify type of data: %, frequency, rate, duration, etc.): <90% accurate, 3 different containers

Current **Stimulus Control**: Needs full physical prompting	Long-term **cue**: Container of liquid, empty glass
Discrete Trial format: No [maximum # per set]	Sequential format: Yes Chained?: Backward Chain

One vs. Two person prompt?: **One**	**Prompt Strategy**: Fade prompt at target step Pause interval (for hierarchy or delayed):

Error Correction: Backstep if not on target step

Natural or additional completion R+: natural: gets a drink, praise	2nd R+ (during task): praise (" Terrific pouring the juice.")
Current 2nd R+ schedule: intermittent praise throughout task	Goal 2nd R+ schedule: praise at the end of the task

Generalization (**stimulus factors**): [people, place, materials, supervision, etc.] Vary staff, location, containers, size of containers, liquid in containers and glasses, size of cups/glasses, fade proximity	Generalization (**response factors**): [rate, accuracy, magnitude, duration, etc.] Reduce the rate at which the task is completed

Parametric details: Fully prompt the student through the task analysis until the last step. Use the necessary prompt for teaching the target step. Once he/she has 3 independent trials on the target step, add the second to last step to the sequence. Allow the student to complete the remaining step(s) independently. Continue with this pattern for the entire task analysis. Note: partial verbal and verbal prompts are not options in the 'prompt level key'.

Task Analysis Data Collection

Steps Date:										
1. Open the container to pouring position										
2. Pick up the container with 2 hands.										
3. Pour liquid into a glass										
4. Stop pouring once you reach the top of the glass										
5. Put the container down										
6. Close the top of the container so that no liquid will get out										
Total										
Staff										

Response Key

Correct: +
Incorrect: -
No response: NR

100										
90										
80										
70										
60										
50										
40										
30										
20										
10										
Date										

Prompt Level Key

FP = full physical
PP = partial physical
M = model
G = gesture
PV = partial verbal
FV = full verbal

Sequential Lesson Plan	Target Skill:	Put on coat

Student:	Teacher:	Date:

Behavior objective: When going outside, the student will put on his/her coat.

Functional association: Domain: Self Help   Function: independent living skills

Current lesson status [acquisition, fluency, maintenance]: fluency
(trials/set; # data-points collected per week): 1 trial/set, 3 data points per week
Target Criterion (specify type of data: %, frequency, rate, duration, etc.): 90% independence of task analysis across 2 staff

Current **Stimulus Control**: Needs partial prompting	Long-term **cue**: Going outside
Discrete Trial format: No [maximum # per set]	Sequential format: Yes Chained?: Backward Chain

One vs. Two person prompt?: **One**	**Prompt Strategy**: Fade Physical Prompt Pause interval (for hierarchy or delayed):

Error Correction: Backstep if not on target step

Natural or additional completion R+: natural: going outside, praise	2nd R+ (during task): praise: ("Great job putting your arm through the sleeve.")
Current 2nd R+ schedule: 1:1 edible for each step	Goal 2nd R+ schedule: fade edible
Generalization (**stimulus factors**): [people, place, materials, etc.] Vary staff, location (e.g., gym, classroom, home), coat (e.g., snap or zip), fade proximity to student as he/she becomes more independent	Generalization (**response factors**): [rate, accuracy, magnitude, duration, etc.] Increase the rate at which the student puts on his/her coat

Parametric details: When it is time to go outside, the student will learn to put on his/her coat. Fully prompt the student through the task analysis except the last step. Provide the necessary prompt for the student to complete this target step. Once the student completes this step three consecutive times independently, then add the second to last step to the sequence. Again provide the necessary prompt for the student to complete this target step. Allow the student to complete the remaining step(s) independently. Indicate a + for an independent response or indicate the level of prompting needed for other responses. Note: partial verbal and verbal prompts are not options in the 'prompt level key'.

Task Analysis

Steps Date:												
1. Pick up coat with opening toward body												
2. Hold coat with left hand above sleeve on the left												
3. Put right arm into sleeve below left hand												
4. Place left arm into other sleeve												
5. Bring coat onto shoulders												
6. Zip or snap												
Total												
Staff:												

Response Key	100										**Prompt Level Key**
	90										
	80										
Correct: +	70										FP = full physical
Incorrect: -	60										PP = partial physical
No response: NR	50										M = model
	40										G = gesture
	30										PV = partial verbal
	20										FV = full verbal
	10										
	Date										

Sequential Lesson Plan	Target Skill:	Put on shoes

Student:	Teacher:	Date:

Behavior objective: After specific activities (e.g., water play, ball pit, and dressing for dramatic play), the student will put on his/her shoes.
Functional association: Domain: Self Help   Function: independent living skills

Current lesson status [acquisition, fluency, maintenance]: acquisition
(trials/set; # data-points collected per week): 3 data points per week
Target Criterion (specify type of data: %, frequency, rate, duration, etc.): 85% of task analysis, 3 staff, 3 pairs of shoes

Current **Stimulus Control**: Needs full physical prompting	Long-term **cue**: Completion of activity done without shoes

Discrete Trial format: No [maximum # per set]	Sequential format: Yes Chained?: Forward Chain

One vs. Two person prompt?: **One**	**Prompt Strategy**: Prompt Hierarchy - FP, PP, G Pause interval (for hierarchy or delayed): 5 seconds

Error Correction: Continued Prompt Hierarchy on target step. Backstep if not on target step

Natural or additional completion R+: praise, small edible	2nd R+ (during task): praise("Good picking up your shoe!")
Current 2nd R+ schedule: praise for step being taught and steps completed independently, small edible upon completion of task	Goal 2nd R+ schedule: praise upon completion of task, fade out edible

Generalization (**stimulus factors**): [people, place, materials, supervision, etc.] Vary activities, shoes, location, and staff, fade staff proximity	Generalization (**response factors**): [rate, accuracy, magnitude, duration, etc.] Decrease amount of time given to complete the task

Parametric details: Upon completion of a shoeless activity (e.g., after playing in the ball pit, changing back into his/her own clothes after dramatic play), the student should get his/her shoes and put them on. Teach target step (1) using the prompt hierarchy and then fully prompt him/her through the remainder of the steps. When the criterion is attained, add teaching the second step using the prompt hierarchy and continue to prompt through the remaining steps. Allow student to complete steps independently prior to target steps. Note: partial verbal and verbal prompts are not an option in the 'prompt level key'.

Task Analysis Data Collection

Steps Date:															
1. Pick up shoe															
2. Pull tongue forward															
3. Lift appropriate foot															
4. Slide toes into shoe															
5. Put foot and shoe on floor															
6. Hold back of shoe with other hand															
7. Push heel down into shoe															
Total															
Staff															

Response Key

Correct: +
Incorrect: -
No response: NR

100											
90											
80											
70											
60											
50											
40				.							
30											
20											
10											
Date											

Prompt Level Key

FP = full physical
PP = partial physical
M = model
G = gesture
PV = partial verbal
FV = full verbal

Sequential Lesson Plan	Target Skill:	Tie shoes

Student:	Teacher:	Date:

Behavior objective: At arranged and/or naturally occurring times, the student will tie his/her shoes.

Functional association: Domain: Self Help   Function: independent living skills, fine motor skills

Current lesson status [acquisition, fluency, maintenance]: acquisition
(trials/set; # data-points collected per week): 3 data points per week
Target Criterion (specify type of data: %, frequency, rate, duration, etc.): <1 prompt across 3 staff

Current **Stimulus Control**: Needs full physical prompting	Long-term **cue**: Untied shoe(s)

Discrete Trial format: No [maximum # per set]	Sequential format: Yes Chained?: Backward Chain

One vs. Two person prompt?: **One**	**Prompt Strategy**: Fading (at target step) Pause interval (for hierarchy or delayed):

Error Correction: Backstep if not on target step

Natural or additional completion R+: praise, gets to go to recess or gym	2nd R+ (during task): praise ("Great pulling the strings tightly.")
Current 2nd R+ schedule: praise, edible	Goal 2nd R+ schedule: praise at completion of task

Generalization (**stimulus factors**): [people, place, materials, supervision, etc.] Vary staff, location, activities shoe tying precedes, types of shoes, and fade staff proximity for independent steps	Generalization (**response factors**): [rate, accuracy, magnitude, duration, etc.] Decrease time it takes to complete steps/task

Parametric details: Set up opportunities for the student to change/put on his/her shoes before/after activities such as gym, swimming, and recess. Also, teach at naturally occurring times when his/her shoes become untied. Fully physical prompt through all steps until the last step. Teach this step using the prompt hierarchy. Indicate the level of prompt required to complete the target step. Once he/she is 80% accurate on the target step, add the prior step to the sequence. Allow the student to complete the remainder of the steps independently.

Task Analysis Data Collection

Steps	Date:												
1. Pick up both strings													
2. Cross one string over the other													
3. Hold crossed strings with one hand													
4. Tuck string into hole with other													
5. Pull both strings tightly													
6. Pick up one string in middle													
7. Grab ends with other finger to make a loop													
8. Wrap string around loop													
9. Tuck part of string in hole													
10. Pull both loops tight													
Total													
Staff													

Response Key

Correct: +
Incorrect: -
No response: NR

100											
90											
80											
70											
60											
50											
40											
30											
20											
10											
Date											

Prompt Level Key

FP = full physical
PP = partial physical
M = model
G = gesture
PV = partial verbal
FV = full verbal

Sequential Lesson Plan	Target Skill:	Undress 1

Student:	Teacher:	Date:

Behavior objective: At specified times (e.g., before and after gym or recess), the student will get undressed.
Functional association: Domain: Self Help   Function: independent living skills

Current lesson status [acquisition, fluency, maintenance]: fluency
(trials/set; # data-points collected per week): 2 per week
Target Criterion (specify type of data: %, frequency, rate, duration, etc.): 90% of TA across 3 trials

Current **Stimulus Control**: Needs prompting (level may vary between gesture and partial physical prompts)	Long-term **cue**: "Change" as indicated on picture schedule

Discrete Trial format: No [maximum # per set]	Sequential format: Yes Chained?: Backward Chain

One vs. Two person prompt?: **One**	**Prompt Strategy:** Fade prompt at target step Pause interval (for hierarchy or delayed):

Error Correction: Backstep if not on target step

Natural or additional completion R+: natural: goes to gym or recess, praise	2nd R+ (during task): praise ("Nice job taking your shoes off.")
Current 2nd R+ schedule: praise 1:3 (every 3 steps)	Goal 2nd R+ schedule: praise at completion of task

Generalization (**stimulus factors**): [people, place, materials, supervision, etc.] Vary staff, clothes, location (e.g., bathroom, classroom, home), and fade staff proximity	Generalization (**response factors**): [rate, accuracy, magnitude, duration, etc.] Increase rate from 10 seconds per item to 3 seconds per item

Parametric details: Once the student sees "change" on his/her schedule, he/she should obtain basket for clothes. A chair should be available for the student to sit on for shoe removal. The student can also sit on the floor if he/she chooses. Provide needed physical or gestural prompts for teaching target step. Avoid verbal prompts. For getting dressed (see "Dressing" lesson plan).

Steps Date:																	
1. Gets the basket for clothes																	
2. Takes off shoe # 1																	
3. Takes off shoe #2																	
4. Pulls arm #1 out of sleeve																	
5. Pulls arm #2 out of sleeve																	
6. Pulls shirt over head																	
7. Stands up																	
8. Grasps pants at waist																	
9. Pulls pants down																	
10. Sits down																	
11. Pulls leg # out																	
12. Pulls leg #2 out																	
Total																	
Staff																	

Response Key	100													**Prompt Level Key**
	90													
	80													
Correct: +	70													FP = full physical
	60													PP = partial physical
Incorrect: -	50													M = model
No response: NR	40													
	30													G = gesture
	20													PV = partial verbal
	10													FV = full verbal
	Date													

Sequential Lesson Plan	Target Skill:	Undress 2

Student:	Teacher:	Date:

Behavior objective: At specified times (e.g., before and after gym or recess), the student will get undressed.
Functional association: Domain: Self Help   Function: independent living skills, fine motor skills

Current lesson status [acquisition, fluency, maintenance]: acquisition
(trials/set; # data-points collected per week): 2 per week
Target Criterion (specify type of data: %, frequency, rate, duration, etc.): 90% of TA across 3 trials

Current **Stimulus Control**: Needs partial to full physical prompting	Long-term **cue**: Going to gym or recess

Discrete Trial format: No [maximum # per set]	Sequential format: Yes Chained?: Backward Chain

One vs. Two person prompt?: **One**	**Prompt Strategy**: Fade prompt at target step Pause interval (for hierarchy or delayed):

Error Correction: Backstep if not on target step

Natural or additional completion R+: natural: goes to gym or recess, praise, small edible	2nd R+ (during task): praise ("Nice job taking your shirt off.")
Current 2nd R+ schedule: edible after every 2 steps, praise after every 4 steps	Goal 2nd R+ schedule: edible at completion of task, praise after independent steps
Generalization (**stimulus factors**): [people, place, materials, etc.] Vary staff, clothes, location (e.g., bathroom, classroom), activities that require changing, and fade staff proximity as student becomes more independent	Generalization (**response factors**): [rate, accuracy, magnitude, duration, etc.] Increase rate from 2 minutes per item to <1 minute per item

Parametric details: The student should begin to get undressed as soon as the basket of clothes is handed to him/her. Staff will complete all steps of the task analysis except the target step. Teach this by fading physical and gestural prompts. Once he/she has 3 consecutive correct responses, add the prior step to the sequence. The student should continue to complete the remaining step(s) independently. Note: partial verbal and verbal prompts are not options in the 'prompt level key'.

Task Analysis

Steps Date											
PANTS											
1. Hold pants at waist											
2. Pull pants down											
3. Sit down											
4. Hold end of one pant leg with one hand and remove foot											
5. Hold other end of pant leg and remove second foot											
SHIRT											
1. Hold sleeve with one hand											
2. Pull sleeve off											
3. Pull shirt over head											
4. Pull shirt off arm #2											
Total											
Staff											

Response Key	100										**Prompt Level Key**
	90										
	80										
Correct: +	70										FP = full physical
Incorrect: -	60										PP = partial physical
No response: NR	50										M = model
	40										G = gesture
	30										PV = partial verbal
	20										FV = full verbal
	10										
	Date										

Sequential Lesson Plan	Target Skill:	Undress 3

Student:	Teacher:	Date:

Behavior objective: At specified times (e.g., before and after gym or recess), the student will get undressed.
Functional association: Domain: Self Help   Function: independent living skills

Current lesson status [acquisition, fluency, maintenance]: acquisition
(trials/set; # data-points collected per week): 2 per week
Target Criterion (specify type of data: %, frequency, rate, duration, etc.): 90% of TA across 3 staff

Current **Stimulus Control**: Needs full physical prompts	Long-term **cue**: Gym or recess

Discrete Trial format: No [maximum # per set]	Sequential format: Yes Chained?: Backward Chain

One vs. Two person prompt?: **One**	**Prompt Strategy**: Fade prompt at target step Pause interval (for hierarchy or delayed):

Error Correction: Backstep if not on target step

Natural or additional completion R+: natural: goes to gym or recess, praise, edible	2nd R+ (during task): praise ("Nice job taking your shoes off.")
Current 2nd R+ schedule: edible at the completion of each item, praise after every 3 steps	Goal 2nd R+ schedule: edible after independent steps only, praise at completion of task
Generalization (**stimulus factors**): [people, place, materials, supervision, etc.] Vary staff, clothes, location (e.g., bathroom, classroom), activities requiring changing, and fade staff proximity	Generalization (**response factors**): [rate, accuracy, magnitude, duration, etc.] Increase rate from 2 minutes per item to < 1 minute per item

Parametric details: The student will begin changing once he/she receives the basket of clothes. Fully prompt (avoid verbal prompts) to last step. Teach this by fading physical and gestural prompts. Once the student has 3 independent responses add the second to last step to the sequence. Allow student to complete remaining steps independently.

Task Analysis Data Collection

	Steps Date														
SHOES	1. Hold heel of shoe with both hands														
	2. Pull shoe over heel														
	3. Pull shoe off														
	4. Hold heel of shoe #2														
	5. Pull shoe over heel														
	6. Pull shoe off														
SOCKS	1. Hold sock at top and back														
	2. Push sock over heel														
	3. Push sock off foot														
	4. Hold sock at top and back														
	5. Push sock over heel														
	6. Push sock off foot														
	Total														
	Staff														

Response Key

Correct: +
Incorrect: -
No response: NR

100													
90													
80													
70													
60													
50													
40													
30													
20													
10													
Date													

Prompt Level Key

FP = full physical
PP = partial physical
M = model
G = gesture
PV = partial verbal
FV = full verbal

Sequential Lesson Plan	Target Skill:	Utensil use 1

Student:	Teacher:	Date:

Behavior objective: During snacks and meals, the student will use one hand to put his/her utensil with food into his/her mouth.

Functional association: Domain: Self Help   Function: independent living skills, social skills

Current lesson status [acquisition, fluency, maintenance]: acquisition
(trials/set; # data-points collected per week):5-10 trials/set, 10-15 data points per week
Target Criterion (specify type of data: %, frequency, rate, duration, etc.): < 1 prompt/5 opportunities, 3 staff, 3 foods

Current **Stimulus Control**: Needs full physical prompting	Long-term **cue**: Food and an eating utensil

Discrete Trial format: No [maximum # per set]	Sequential format: Yes Chained?: No

One vs. Two person prompt?: **One**	**Prompt Strategy**: Graduated Guidance (hand over hand, hand over wrist, hand over lower arm, hand over elbow, hand over upper arm)

Error Correction: Backstep if not on target step, but prompting strategy stated should avoid errors

Natural or additional completion R+: natural: eats food, praise	2nd R+ (during task): praise ("Great using one hand to eat!")
Current 2nd R+ schedule:1:1 praise for independent trials	Goal 2nd R+ schedule: 1:3 praise for independent trials

Generalization (**stimulus factors**): [people, place, materials, supervision, etc.] Vary staff, foods eaten (e.g., pudding, yogurt, cereal, and vegetables), utensils used (e.g., spoon or fork), location, time of day, and fade proximity as the student becomes more independent with the task	Generalization (**response factors**): [rate, accuracy, magnitude, duration, etc.] Decrease time taken to complete meals if appropriate

Parametric details: The student should use one hand to scoop up the food with the utensil, bring the food toward and into his/her mouth. Stand behind the student and fully prompt him/her through the task. As the student becomes more independent with the steps, fade your hand placement as listed above in the prompt strategy. Avoid verbal prompts. Fade assistance when the student begins to complete steps 2 and 3 independently.

Task Analysis

Steps Date:												
1. Scoops food onto utensil												
2. Brings utensil to mouth (using one hand)												
3. Puts utensil and food into mouth (using one hand)												
Total												
Staff												

Response Key	100											**Prompt Level Key**
	90											
	80											
Correct: +	70											FP = full physical
Incorrect: -	60											PP = partial physical
No response: NR	50											M = model
	40											G = gesture
	30											PV = partial verbal
.	20											FV = full verbal
	10											
	Date											

Pyramid Educational Consultants

Sequential Lesson Plan	Target Skill:	Utensil use 2

Student:	Teacher:	Date:

Behavior objective: During snacks and meals, the student will use one hand to put his utensil and food into his/her mouth.
Functional association: Domain: Self Help   Function: independent living skills, social skills

Current lesson status [acquisition, fluency, maintenance]: fluency
(trials/set; # data-points collected per week): 5-10 trials/set, 10-15 data points per week
Target Criterion (specify type of data: %, frequency, rate, duration, etc.) < 1 prompt/5 opportunities, 3 staff, 6 foods

Current **Stimulus Control**: Needs a model	Long-term **cue**: Food and an eating utensil

Discrete Trial format: No [maximum # per set]	Sequential format: Yes Chained?: No

One vs. Two person prompt?: **One**	**Prompt Strategy**: Prompt Hierarchy - G, PP, FP Pause interval (for hierarchy or delayed): 3 seconds

Error Correction: Backstep

Natural or additional completion R+: natural: eats food, praise	2nd R+ (during task): praise ("Great using one hand to eat!")
Current 2nd R+ schedule: 1:1 praise for independent trials	Goal 2nd R+ schedule: 1:5 praise for independent trials

Generalization (**stimulus factors**): [people, place, materials, supervision, etc.] Vary staff, foods (e.g., pudding, yogurt, cereal, and vegetables), utensil used (e.g., spoon or fork), location, time of day, and fade staff proximity as the student becomes more independent with the task	Generalization (**response factors**): [rate, accuracy, magnitude, duration, etc.] Decrease time needed to complete meal (if appropriate)

Parametric details: The student should use one hand to scoop up the food with the utensil, bring the food toward and into his/her mouth. If the student tries to use his/her second hand, gently block the response. Next, empty the utensil of food, the student should then re-scoop the food onto the utensil and lift toward the mouth with one hand. If needed, gently hold second hand down. For each trial, record "+" if the student eats using one hand independently or "-" if he/she requires a prompt. Avoid verbal prompts.

Data Collection

Date	Staff	+/-	Comments

Response Key													**Prompt Level Key**
	100												
	90												
	80												
Correct: +	70												FP = full physical
	60												PP = partial physical
Incorrect: -	50												M = model
No response: NR	40												
	30												G = gesture
	20												PV = partial verbal
	10												FV = full verbal
	Date												

Sequential Lesson Plan	Target Skill:	Wash face

Student:	Teacher:	Date:

Behavior objective: When the student's face is dirty, he/she will wash it.
Functional association: Domain: Self Help   Function: independent living skill, hygiene

Current lesson status [acquisition, fluency, maintenance]: acquisition
(trials/set; # data-points collected per week): 1 trial/set, 1data point per week
Target Criterion (specify type of data: %, frequency, rate, duration, etc.): 80% accuracy across 3 days

Current **Stimulus Control**: Picture of wash face on schedule following meals, partial physical prompting	Long-term **cue**: Dirty face
Discrete Trial format: No [maximum # per set]	Sequential format: Yes Chained?: Backward Chain
One vs. Two person prompt?: **One**	**Prompt Strategy**: Fade prompt at target step **Pause interval (for hierarchy or delayed)**:

Error Correction: Backstep if not on target step

Natural or additional completion R+: praise, edible/token	2nd R+ (during task): praise ("Great turning on the water!")
Current 2nd R+ schedule: 1:3 praise, edible	Goal 2nd R+ schedule: praise at end of task
Generalization (**stimulus factors**): [people, place, materials, supervision, etc.] Vary staff, locations (e.g., home bathroom, school bathroom, kitchen sink), times of day, and materials	Generalization (**response factors**): [rate, accuracy, magnitude, duration, etc.] Decrease amount of time given to complete steps of task

Parametric details: After meals (as indicated on picture schedule), the student will wash his/her face. Other chances include before bedtime and after waking up in the morning. Staff will prompt (no verbals) the student through the entire sequence and then use the necessary prompts to teach the target step. After 3 days of independent responses on the last step, add the second to last step to the sequence. Continue this pattern for all steps, maintaining independent steps.

Task Analysis
1. Get basket of materials and bring to bathroom.
2. Pick up wash cloth
3. Turn on the water
4. Wet the wash cloth
5. Pick up the soap from the basket
6. Rub the soap on the cloth
7. Put the soap back in the basket
8. Wash forehead, nose, chin
9. Wash cheeks
10. Turn on water
11. Rinse cloth
12. Squeeze excess water out of cloth
13. Rinse forehead, nose, chin
14. Rinse cheeks
15. Rinse cloth
16. Put cloth in basket
17. Get paper towel
18. Dry face with paper towel
19. Throw paper towel away
20. Return basket to shelf

Target Step	Date												
Total:													
Staff:													

Response Key

Correct: +
Incorrect: -
No response: NR

100										
90										
80										
70										
60										
50										
40										
30										
20										
10										
Date										

Prompt Level Key

FP = full physical
PP = partial physical
M = model
G = gesture
PV = partial verbal
FV = full verbal

Sequential Lesson Plan	Target Skill:	Wash hands	

Student:	Teacher:	Date:

Behavior objective: Before mealtime or when his/her hands are dirty, the student will wash his/her hands.
Functional association: Domain: Self Help   Function: independent living, hygiene

Current lesson status [acquisition, fluency, maintenance]: acquisition
(trials/set; # data-points collected per week): 3 created opportunities/day, 2 data points/week
Target Criterion (specify type of data : %, frequency, rate, duration, etc.): 80% accuracy across 3 days

Current **Stimulus Control**: Needs partial physical prompting	Long-term **cue**: Wash hands before meals and when dirty
Discrete Trial format: No [maximum # per set]	Sequential format: Yes Chained?: Backward Chain

One vs. Two person prompt?: **One**	**Prompt Strategy**: Fade prompt at target step **Pause interval (for hierarchy or delayed):**

Error Correction: Backstep if not on target step

Natural or additional completion R+: natural: meals	2nd R+ (during task): praise (" Nice washing hands.")
Current 2nd R+ schedule: intermittent praise throughout task	Goal 2nd R+ schedule: praise at end of task

Generalization (**stimulus factors**): [people, place, materials, supervision, etc.] Vary staff, sinks, bathrooms, soap and towels, fade staff proximity as independence increases	Generalization (**response factors**): [rate, accuracy, magnitude, duration, etc.] Decrease amount of time needed to complete task

Parametric details: The student will wash his/her hands before meals and after messy activities. Such activities may include but are not limited to: painting, cooking, playing outside, planting, and toileting. Begin by fully prompting the student through the entire task analysis until the last step. Teach the target step by providing the necessary physical or gestural prompt (avoiding verbal prompts). Once independent, add the second to the last step to the sequence. Again, teach this step by providing the necessary prompt while allowing the student to complete the remaining step(s) independently. Continue this procedure until the student can complete all steps of the task analysis independently.

Task Analysis

1. Approach sink	5. Put hand under soap dispenser	9. Turn water off
2. Turn on water	6. Push dispenser with other hand	10. Get paper towel
3. Wet hand #1	7. Rub hands together	11. Dry hands with towel
4. Wet hand #2	8. Rinse hands	12. Throw towel away

Target Step	Date											
Total:												
Staff:												

Response Key

Correct: +
Incorrect: -
No response: NR

100											
90											
80											
70											
60											
50											
40											
30											
20											
10											
Date											

Prompt Level Key

FP = full physical
PP = partial physical
M = model
G = gesture
PV = partial verbal
FV = full verbal

Sequential Lesson Plan	Target Skill:	Zip coat

Student:	Teacher:	Date:

Behavior objective: Before going outside, the student will zipper his/her coat.

Functional association: Domain: Self Help   Function: independent living skills, eye-hand coordination

Current lesson status [acquisition, fluency, maintenance]: acquisition
(trials/set; # data-points collected per week): 1 trial/set, 3 data points/week
Target Criterion (specify type of data: %, frequency, rate, duration, etc.): <90% of TA across 2 coats

Current **Stimulus Control**: Needs full physical prompting	Long-term **cue**: Going outside

Discrete Trial format: No [maximum # per set]	Sequential format: Yes Chained?: Backward Chain

One vs. Two person prompt?: **One**	**Prompt Strategy**: Fade prompt at target step Pause interval (for hierarchy or delayed)

Error Correction : Backstep if not on target step

Natural or additional completion R+: natural: going outside	2nd R+ (during task): social praise: (" Nice putting on your coat.")

Current 2nd R+ schedule: intermittent praise	Goal 2nd R+ schedule: praise at the completion of the task

Generalization (**stimulus factors**): [people, place, materials, supervision, etc.] Vary staff, locations, coats, time of day (e.g., before recess, going home, field trips), and increase proximity as the student increases independence	Generalization (**response factors**): [rate, accuracy, magnitude, duration, etc.] Decrease amount of time it takes the student to zipper as accuracy on task increase

Parametric details: The student will work on zippering his/her coat before going outside (e.g., playground, bus, home, walk). Staff will fully prompt him/her through the task analysis until the last step. Staff should use the needed prompt to teach the target step. Once the student meets criteria for this step add the prior step to the sequence, again using the necessary prompt to teach this step. Allow the student to complete the remaining step(s) independently. Continue to add additional steps to the sequence as the student demonstrates criteria. Note: partial verbal and verbal prompts are not options in the 'prompt level key'.

Task Analysis Data Collection

Steps	Date:											
1. Hold one end of the jacket with one hand												
2. Hold the other end with the other hand												
3. Bring the two ends together and insert the zipper												
4. Hold the zipper in one hand												
5. Hold the end of the jacket with the other hand												
6. Pull the zipper up to chest area												
Total												
Staff												

Response Key

Correct: +
Incorrect: -
No response: NR

100											
90											
80											
70											
60											
50											
40											
30											
20											
10											
Date											

Prompt Level Key

FP = full physical
PP = partial physical
M = model
G = gesture
PV = partial verbal
FV = full verbal

Social Lesson Plans

Discrete Lesson Plan	Target Skill:	Follow one step directions from peer

Student:	Teacher:	Date:

Behavior objective: During group activities, the student will follow one step directions from his/her peers.
Functional association: Domain: Social   Function: communication, direction following

Current lesson status [acquisition, fluency, maintenance]: fluency
(trials/set; # data-points collected per week): 3 data points per week
Target Criterion (specify type of data: %, frequency, rate, duration, etc.): <1 prompt/5 opportunities across 2 peers

Current **Stimulus Control**: Needs gesture to partial physical prompt	Long-term **cue**: Peer directive

Discrete Trial format: Yes [maximum # per set] 3/interaction	Sequential format: No Chained?: No

One vs. Two person prompt?: Two (Peer and Teacher)	**Prompt Strategy**: Fading - FP, PP, G Pause interval (for hierarchy or delayed):

Error Correction: Provide sufficient prompt level

Natural or additional completion R+: praise, continue activity or access to next	2nd R+ (during task): praise ("Great following the direction.")
Current 2nd R+ schedule: 1:1 praise from peer ("Great job giving me the ball.")	Goal 2nd R+ schedule: 1:4 praise

Generalization (**stimulus factors**): [people, place, materials, supervision, etc.] Vary staff, peers, locations, activities, directions given (e.g., give me the ball, move your piece here, color this red), and fade staff proximity	Generalization (**response factors**): [rate, accuracy, magnitude, duration, etc.] Increase complexity of direction

Parametric details: Select directions to which the student correctly responds when given by a teacher/staff member. Work on this skill with regular education "buddies" during Reverse Mainstreaming activities such as games and crafts. Staff should stand behind the student and prompt him/her from behind. Staff should fade prompts and proximity over time. Peer should immediately provide reinforcement. Indicate level of prompt given or if the student followed the direction independently.

Data Collection

Date	Staff	Peer	Direction given	Date	Staff	Peer	Direction given	Comments

Response Key	100											**Prompt Level Key**
	90											
	80											
Correct: +	70											FP = full physical
Incorrect: -	60											PP = partial physical
No response: NR	50											M = model
	40											G = gesture
	30											PV = partial verbal
	20											FV = full verbal
	10											
	Date											

Discrete Lesson Plan	Target Skill:	Greeting peers upon entering

Student:	Teacher:	Date:

Behavior objective: When seeing a peer enter an area for the first time that day, the student will say, "Hi, _____."
Functional association: Domain: Social   Function: communication, social skills

Current lesson status [acquisition, fluency, maintenance]: acquisition
(trials/set; # data-points collected per week): 2 created or spontaneous/day
Target Criterion (specify type of data: %, frequency, rate, duration, etc.): <1 prompt/5 opportunities

Current **Stimulus Control**: Needs a model	Long-term cue: Seeing peer enter a room or area

Discrete Trial format: Yes [maximum # per set] 1trial/set	Sequential format: No Chained?: No

One vs. Two person prompt?: **One**	**Prompt Strategy**: Delayed prompting (to Model) *Pause interval (for hierarchy or delayed):* 1 second progressive time delay (max. 5 sec.)

Error Correction: Shorten next delay (Note: if model fails, use 4-step switch for imitation)

Natural or additional completion R+: natural: peer responds, praise, small edible	2nd R+ (during task): n/a
Current 2nd R+ schedule: 1:1 praise: ("Nice saying hi to John.") 1:1 small edible	Goal 2nd R+ schedule: 1:3 praise, fade out edible

Generalization (**stimulus factors**): [people, place, materials, supervision, etc.] Vary staff, location, peers, adults, time of day, and fade staff proximity as the student begins to initiate greetings independently	Generalization (**response factors**): [rate, accuracy, magnitude, duration, etc.] Work on other greetings such as, "Hey," "How are ya?," and "What's up?"

Parametric details: Practice greetings throughout the day by arranging for peers to enter student's area. Begin with immediate model of greeting to peer. If the student imitates, peer provides greeting and praise. If no imitation, teacher uses 4-step EC to get imitation (followed by peer reinforcement). Increase delay between peer entering and model by 1 second increments (after 5 consecutive +'s). Indicate whether the student successfully imitates the model. If the student initiates the greeting without a model, indicate this with a "+" in the designated column below. Also, note the initiated greeting form.

Data Collection

Date	Staff	Peer	Phrase modeled/initiated	Imitates (+/-)	Initiates (+)	Comments

Response Key

Correct: +
Incorrect: -
No response: NR

100										
90										
80										
70										
60										
50										
40										
30										
20										
10										
Date										

Prompt Level Key

FP = full physical
PP = partial physical
M = model
G = gesture
PV = partial verbal
FV = full verbal

Pyramid Educational Consultants

Discrete Lesson Plan	Target Skill:	Initiate gestural greeting

Student:	Teacher:	Date:

Behavior objective: Upon encountering someone for the first time that day, the student will wave "hi" to that person.

Functional association: Domain: Social   Function: social skills, communication

Current lesson status [acquisition, fluency, maintenance]: acquisition
(trials/set; # data-points collected per week):1 trial/set, 3 data points/week
Target Criterion (specify type of data: %, frequency, rate, duration, etc.): 4/5 trials without prompting, across 4 people

Current **Stimulus Control**: Needs a model	Long-term **cue**: A person in an entered room or area

Discrete Trial format: Yes [maximum # per set] 1trial/set	Sequential format: No Chained?: No

One vs. Two person prompt?: **Two**	**Prompt Strategy**: Graduated Guidance - hand over hand, hand on wrist, hand on forearm, hand on upper arm, hand on shoulder Pause interval (for hierarchy or delayed):

Error Correction: Provide sufficient prompt level

Natural or additional completion R+: praise and access to next activity, edible	2nd R+ (during task): praise ("Great waving your hand hi.")
Current 2nd R+ schedule: 1:1 edible, 1:1praise	Goal 2nd R+ schedule: praise only

Generalization (**stimulus factors**): [people, place, materials, supervision, etc.] Vary staff, locations (e.g., cafeteria, gym, hallway), fade staff proximity as independence increases	Generalization (**response factors**): [rate, accuracy, magnitude, duration, etc.] Differentiate responses - thumbs up, hi-5, hand shake

Parametric details: Upon entering an area and seeing someone for the first time that day, the physical prompter (person behind student) will fully prompt him/her to wave his/her hand. The physical prompter gradually fades the level of prompting and proximity needed. The person greeted (not the prompter) responds with a greeting and praise.

Data Collection

Date	Staff	Person greeted	Prompt level	Comments			

Response Key

Correct: +
Incorrect: -
No response: NR

100											
90											
80											
70											
60											
50											
40											
30											
20											
10											
Date											

Prompt Level Key

FP = full physical
PP = partial physical
M = model
G = gesture
PV = partial verbal
FV = full verbal

Sequential Lesson Plan	Target Skill:	**Request from peer with PECS**

Student:	Teacher:	Date:

Behavior objective: During group activities, the student will request items from peers.

Functional association: Domain: Social   Function: requesting items from peers, social interaction

Current lesson status [acquisition, fluency, maintenance]: acquisition
(trials/set; # data-points collected per week): 5 data points per week
Target Criterion (specify type of data: %, frequency, rate, duration, etc.): 85% accuracy across 3 peers

Current **Stimulus Control**: Full and partial prompting	Long-term **cue**: Item

Discrete Trial format: No [maximum # per set]	Sequential format: Yes Chained?: Backward Chain

One vs. Two person prompt?: Two (Peer and Teacher)	**Prompt Strategy**: Prompt Hierarchy Fading - FP, PP, G Pause interval (for hierarchy or delayed):

Error Correction: Provide prompt level needed

Natural or additional completion R+: natural: receiving needed or wanted item	2nd R+ (during task): praise ("Great job asking for the scissors."), token
Current 2nd R+ schedule: 1:1 praise, 1:1 token	Goal 2nd R+ schedule: 1:3 praise, 1:4 token
Generalization (**stimulus factors**): [people, place, materials, supervision, etc.] Vary staff, settings, materials, and activities (e.g., art, snack, games), peers and fade staff proximity	Generalization (**response factors**): [rate, accuracy, magnitude, duration, etc.] Increase number of requested items

Parametric details: Full prompt through all steps until the last step. Once 80% accurate on this step then add the prior step to the sequence. Allow the student to complete the remaining step(s) independently. Begin by teaching this lesson during snack and then add arts and crafts. Slowly introduce other activities. Since this lesson involves the use of PECS, the student must be on Phase IV. However, the student can make single picture requests in which case Phase III competency is then the minimal requirement.

Task Analysis Data Collection

Steps	Date:												
1. Open communication book													
2. Put Sentence Strip together for needed/wanted item													
3. Get peer attention													
4. Exchange Sentence Strip with peer													
5. Point/read Sentence Strip													
6. Wait for item to be given													
Total													
Staff													

Response Key

Correct: +
Incorrect: -
No response: NR

100										
90										
80										
70										
60										
50										
40										
30										
20										
10										
Date										

Prompt Level Key

FP = full physical
PP = partial physical
M = model
G = gesture
PV = partial verbal
FV = full verbal

Pyramid Educational Consultants

Discrete Lesson Plan	Target Skill:	Request from peer

Student:	Teacher:	Date:

Behavior objective: Throughout the school day, the student will request items and materials from his/her peers.

Functional association: Domain: Social   Function: social skills, communication, independent work skills

Current lesson status [acquisition, fluency, maintenance]: acquisition
(trials/set; # data-points collected per week):1-3 trials per set, 5 data points per week
Target Criterion (specify type of data: %, frequency, rate, duration, etc.): <1 prompt/5 opportunities, 3 peers, 3 activities

Current **Stimulus Control**: Needs a written prompt	Long-term **cue**: Peer has desired item or materials

Discrete Trial format: Yes [maximum # per set] 1-3 trials/set	Sequential format: No Chained?: No

One vs. Two person prompt?: **One**	**Prompt Strategy**: Fading (written prompt) Pause interval (for hierarchy or delayed):

Error Correction: Use level of written prompt needed

Natural or additional completion R+: natural: gets item or materials requested, praise	2nd R+ (during task): praise ("Excellent asking Kate for the ball!")
Current 2nd R+ schedule: 1:1 praise, 1:1 natural	Goal 2nd R+ schedule: 1:4 praise, 1:1 natural
Generalization (**stimulus factors**): [people, place, materials, supervision, etc.] Vary staff, peers, activities, items, materials to be requested, locations, fade staff proximity	Generalization (**response factors**): [rate, accuracy, magnitude, duration, etc.] Vary number of trials per set, introduce other request forms such as, "Can I have the ____, please." or "____, hand me the ____, please."

Parametric details: Work on this skill across the day during activities such as arts and crafts, snack and meal preparation, lunch, and less structured "free play" time. Place preferred/desired items by peers so that the student must ask for them. Give the student the written prompt, "(Name), I want ____, please." After the student follows this written prompt three times independently, fade out one letter from the end of the sentence. When the student follows this written prompt independently 3 times, fade out one more letter. Continue this protocol until all letters are faded or the student is independently requesting items from peers in the absence of the written prompt.

Data Collection

Date	Staff	Object requested	Which letter dropped?	Followed prompt? (+ / -)	Comments	

Response Key

Correct: +
Incorrect: -
No response: NR

100										
90										
80										
70										
60										
50										
40										
30										
20										
10										
Date										

Prompt Level Key

FP = full physical
PP = partial physical
M = model
G = gesture
PV = partial verbal
FV = full verbal

Discrete Lesson Plan		Target Skill:	Respond to greetings

Student:	Teacher:	Date:

Behavior objective: When an adult says, "Hi" to the student, he/she will respond with a hand wave.

Functional association: Domain: Social   Function: social skills, communication

Current lesson status [acquisition, fluency, maintenance]: acquisition
(trials/set; # data-points collected per week): 1 trial/set, 3 data points/week
Target Criterion (specify type of data: %, frequency, rate, duration, etc.): 2 prompts/5 opportunities, across 3 people

Current **Stimulus Control**: Needs partial to full physical prompting	Long-term **cue**: Greeted

Discrete Trial format: Yes [maximum # per set] 1	Sequential format: No Chained?: No

One vs. Two person prompt?: **Two**	**Prompt Strategy**: Shaping/fading physical prompts Pause interval (for hierarchy or delayed):

Error Correction: Use level of assistance needed

Natural or additional completion R+: praise and continued interaction, edible	2nd R+ (during task): praise ("Great waving your hand hi.")
Current 2nd R+ schedule: 1:1 praise, 1:1 edible	Goal 2nd R+ schedule: praise only

Generalization (**stimulus factors**): [people, place, materials, supervision, etc.] Vary staff, locations (e.g., cafeteria, gym, or hallway), introduce peers, and fade staff proximity	Generalization (**response factors**): [rate, accuracy, magnitude, duration etc.] Differentiate greetings (e.g., "Hey", "Hi", "How are you?")

Parametric details: When someone greets the student by saying "Hi", he/she will respond with a wave of the hand. The physical prompter (person behind the student) will fully prompt him/her to wave his/her hand when greeted. The student will be reinforced with an edible. After 5 trials of fully prompting the student to wave his/her hand, begin to reinforce small approximations of the wave. Reinforce now when the student moves his/her hand by his side. After he/she has 5 successful trials of waving his/her hand by his/her side, then reinforce when his/her hand moves to his/her waist. Follow same protocol for reinforcing at his/her stomach and chest level. State below where his/her hand movement occurred and if the student was reinforced. Do not reinforce if the student waves his/her hand lower than what your present criterion is. Fade physical prompter when the student indicates consistent responses to being greeted.

Data Collection

Date	Staff greeted	Side	Waist	Stomach	Chest	R+?	Comments	

Response Key

Correct: +
Incorrect: -
No response: NR

100										
90										
80										
70										
60										
50										
40										
30										
20										
10										
Date										

Prompt Level Key

FP = full physical
PP = partial physical
M = model
G = gesture
PV = partial verbal
FV = full verbal

Discrete Lesson Plan		Target Skill:	Share toy when asked by peer

Student:	Teacher:	Date:

Behavior objective: Given a toy during playtime, the student will share the toy when asked by a peer.
Functional association: Domain: Social   Function: learning to play appropriately with peers

Current lesson status [acquisition, fluency, maintenance]: fluency
(trials/set; # data-points collected per week): 1 trial/set, 2 data points per week
Target Criterion (specify type of data: %, frequency, rate, duration, etc.): < 2 prompts/5 minutes, 3 peers

Current **Stimulus Control**: Needs partial to full physical prompting to share toy	Long-term **cue**: Toy and peer

Discrete Trial format: Yes [maximum # per set] 1 trial/set	Sequential format: No Chained?: No

One vs. Two person prompt?: **One**	**Prompt Strategy**: Prompt Hierarchy - G, PP, FP Pause interval (for hierarchy or delayed): 3 seconds

Error Correction: Continued Prompt Hierarchy

Natural or additional completion R+: praise, continues with game, earns tokens	2nd R+ (during task): praise ("Wonderful job sharing the toy with Peter!")
Current 2nd R+ schedule: VI 1 min. earning 4 tokens, cash out for small edible or activity after earning 4 tokens, intermittent praise	Goal 2nd R+ schedule: VI 3 min. earning 4 tokens, cash out for small edible or activity after earning 4 tokens, praise 1:2 tokens
Generalization (**stimulus factors**): [people, place, materials, supervision, etc.] Vary peers that the student plays with, vary materials, vary location (e.g., play areas in different classrooms, gym, playground), fade staff proximity	Generalization (**response factors**): [rate, accuracy, magnitude, duration, etc.] Increase duration of toy sharing

Parametric details: Given a toy, such as the garage or marble works, the student will share the toy with his/her peers when asked by a peer. The peer should have independent skills in this area (e.g., can approach peer and ask for a turn, can ask 'can I play with you?', 'can ask can I play with the marble works too?'). Indicate the number of prompts needed to share appropriately. It may be necessary to gradually work towards the 5-minute criteria.

Data Collection

Date	Staff	Peer(s)	Toy(s)	Duration	# of prompts	Comments		

Response Key		**Prompt Level Key**
Correct: + Incorrect: - No response: NR	100 / 90 / 80 / 70 / 60 / 50 / 40 / 30 / 20 / 10 / Date	FP = full physical PP = partial physical M = model G = gesture PV = partial verbal FV = full verbal

Discrete Lesson Plan	Target Skill:	Toy play

Student:	Teacher:	Date:

Behavior objective: During structured playtime, the student will play with age appropriate toy(s) for at least 5 minutes.
Functional association: Domain: Social   Function: social skills, play skills

Current lesson status [acquisition, fluency, maintenance]: acquisition
(trials/set; # data-points collected per week): 1 trial/set, 2 data points per week
Target Criterion (specify type of data: %, frequency, rate, duration, etc.): <2 prompts/5 minutes, 3 toys

Current **Stimulus Control**: Needs gestural to full physical prompting	Long-term **cue**: Toy

Discrete Trial format: Yes [maximum # per set] 1trial/set	Sequential format: No Chained?: No

One vs. Two person prompt?: **One**	Prompt Strategy: Shaping Pause interval (for hierarchy or delayed):

Error Correction: Least intrusive non-verbal prompt back to play

Natural or additional completion R+: praise, continued access to toy, edible given every 20 seconds	2nd R+ (during task): praise ("Nice playing with the toy."), edibles
Current 2nd R+ schedule: praise and edible 1:20 seconds	Goal 2nd R+ schedule: praise completion, eliminate edible

Generalization (**stimulus factors**): [people, place, materials, supervision, etc.] Vary staff, toys (e.g., garage, cars, blocks), locations of play (e.g., classroom, outside, home), fade staff proximity	Generalization (**response factors**): [rate, accuracy, magnitude, duration, etc.] Increase amount of time spent playing with a toy

Parametric details: Begin this lesson once a child has learned how to play with an age appropriate toy. Begin with the student playing with toys for 15 seconds. After 3 trials of < 2 prompts, increase the time interval by 15 second increments. Make sure to vary toys. Initially, toys should be highly preferred and chosen by the student. Count the number of prompts needed to stay on task and play with the toy(s). Reduce rate of praise only after 5 minutes is achieved by increasing intervals in increments of 50% of previous interval.

Data Collection

Date	Staff	# prompts	Duration	Distance	Toy	Rate of praise	Comments

Response Key		**Prompt Level Key**
Correct: + Incorrect: - No response: NR	100 90 80 70 60 50 40 30 20 10 Date	FP = full physical PP = partial physical M = model G = gesture PV = partial verbal FV = full verbal

Sequential Lesson Plan	Target Skill:	Turn taking with visual cues	

Student:	Teacher:	Date:

Behavior objective: During group games, the student will take his/her turn.
Functional association: Domain: Social   Function: recreation/leisure, social skills, waiting for turn

Current lesson status [acquisition, fluency, maintenance]: acquisition
(trials/set; # data-points collected per week): 5 trials/set, 2 data points per week
Target Criterion (specify type of data: %, frequency, rate, duration, etc.): < 1prompt/turn, across 3 games

Current **Stimulus Control**: Needs gestural to full physical prompting	Long-term **cue**: Spinner or bucket is passed to student
Discrete Trial format: No [maximum # per set] 5 trials/set	Sequential format: Yes (repeated) Chained?: No

One vs. Two person prompt?: **One**	**Prompt Strategy**: Least to Most Prompt Hierarchy - G, PP, FP Pause interval (for hierarchy or delayed): 3 seconds

Error Correction: Backstep and increase prompt level

Natural or additional completion R+: intermittent praise throughout the task, edible at the end of the task	2nd R+ (during task): praise ("Good job passing the spinner."), edible
Current 2nd R+ schedule: praise at the end of each turn, edible at the end of each turn after he/she passes the spinner or bucket to the next player	Goal 2nd R+ schedule: praise at the end of 3 turns, fade edible to 1:3 turns
Generalization (**stimulus factors**): [people, place, materials, supervision, etc.] Vary staff, games (e.g., lotto, Teddy Bear Bingo), location (e.g., home, classroom, other classrooms), peers, and fade staff proximity	Generalization (**response factors**): [rate, accuracy, magnitude, duration, etc.] Increase complexity of games

Parametric details: The student will begin by playing a game with one staff and one peer. When the bucket of cards (for lotto game) is passed to him/her, he/she will pick a card, match the card to the same on his/her board, and pass the bucket to the next player. If playing a game with a spinner, then the sequence is: spin the spinner, follow the direction of the spinner, and pass the spinner to the next player. There are a total of 3 prompts that could be given during each turn. Count the # of prompts per turn. Indicate which # (s) were incorrect.

Data Collection

Date	Staff	Peer(s)	Game	# prompts/turn	# missed	Comments

Response Key	100												**Prompt Level Key**
	90												
	80												
Correct: +	70												FP = full physical
Incorrect: -	60												PP = partial physical
	50												
No response: NR	40												M = model
	30												G = gesture
	20												PV = partial verbal
	10												
	Date												FV = full verbal

Appendix

Sequential Lesson Plan	Target Skill:	Make cookies

Student:	Teacher:	Date:

Behavior objective: At scheduled times (e.g., before snacks and meals), the student will make refrigerated dough cookies.

Functional association: Domain: Domestic   Function: independent living skills

Current lesson status [acquisition, fluency, maintenance]: acquisition
(trials/set; # data-points collected per week): 1 data point per week
Target Criterion (specify type of data: %, frequency, rate, duration, etc.): 80% accuracy, across 2 staff, 2 kinds of cookies

Current **Stimulus Control**: Needs gestural to full physical prompting	Long-term **cue**: "Make cookies" as indicated on picture schedule
Discrete Trial format: No [maximum # per set]	Sequential format: Yes Chained?: Backward Chain (repeated)

One vs. Two person prompt?: **One**	**Prompt Strategy**: Most to Least Prompt Hierarchy - FP, PP, G Pause interval (for hierarchy or delayed):

Error Correction: Provide sufficient prompt - increase support level next trial

Natural or additional completion R+: Natural: eats cookies, praise	2nd R+ (during task): praise ("Great job getting the dough.")
Current 2nd R+ schedule: intermittent praise	Goal 2nd R+ schedule: praise at completion of task

Generalization (**stimulus factors**): [people, place, materials, supervision, etc.] Vary type of cookie dough (e.g., chocolate chip, peanut butter), vary staff, vary location (e.g., kitchen at group home, kitchen at school, kitchen at home), fade staff proximity	Generalization (**response factors**): [rate, accuracy, magnitude, duration, etc.] Vary number of cookies made (e.g., make enough for another class, too)

Parametric details: Staff will begin by cutting the end off the cookie dough wrapper. Staff will then physically prompt the student through the first three steps of the sequence. Staff will prompt the student to complete the last step of the sequence. Indicate what prompt level was needed to complete the target step. Once the student can complete this step 4 consecutive times independently, add the second to the last step to the sequence. Allow the student to complete the remaining step(s) independently. Once all the cookie dough is on the tray, staff will put the tray into the oven. When the cookies are done, the student gets to eat them.

Data Collection

Steps Date:	1/1	1/5	1/9	1/15	1/21	1/27	2/2	2/6	2/11	2/20	2/25	3/1	3/5	3/9	3/14
1. Peel plastic from dough	FP	FP	FP	FP	FP	FP	FP	FP	FP	FP	PP	PP	G	+	+
2. Pick up knife	FP	FP	FP	FP	PP	PP	G	PP	G	+	+	+	+	+	+
3. Cut off thin slice of dough	FP	FP	FP	FP	PP	+	+	+	+	+	+	+	+	+	+
4. Place slice on tray	PP	+	+	+	+	+	+	+	+	+	+	+	+	+	+
5. Repeat step 3 until dough is gone	FP	FP	FP	FP	FP	FP	PP	FP	PP	PP	PP	PP	PP	PP	G
Total:	0	20	20	20	20	40	40	40	40	60	60	60	60	80	80
Staff:	IM	SD	GA	SD	KI	GA	HA	GH	IM	IM	SD	IM	KI	GH	SD

Response Key

Correct: +
Incorrect: -
No response: NR

100												
90												
80			.									
70												
60												
50												
40												
30												
20												
10												
Date	1/1	1/5	1/9	1/15	1/21	1/27	2/2	2/6	2/11	2/20	2/25	3/1

Prompt Level Key

FP = full physical
PP = partial physical
M = model
G = gesture
PV = partial verbal
FV = full verbal

Discrete Lesson Plan	Target Skill:	Follow one-step spoken directions

Student:	Teacher:	Date:

Behavior objective: Throughout the day, the student will follow one step verbal directions.
Functional association: Domain: School Based • Function: receptive language, direction following

Current lesson status [acquisition, fluency, maintenance]: acquisition
(trials/set; # data-points collected per week):1 trials/set, 5 data points per week
Target Criterion (specify type of data: %, frequency, rate, duration, etc.): 80% accuracy, 5 directions, 3 staff

Current **Stimulus Control**: Needs full physical prompting	Long-term **cue**: A verbal direction

Discrete Trial format: Yes [maximum # per set] 1 trial/set	Sequential format: No Chained?: No

One vs. Two person prompt? **One**	**Prompt Strategy**: Most to Least Prompt Hierarchy - FP, PP, G Pause interval (for hierarchy or delayed):

Error Correction: Backstep

Natural or additional completion R+: natural: continues with current activity, praise, token	2nd R+ (during task): praise ("Great putting the bottle in the refrigerator."), token
Current 2nd R+ schedule: 1:1 praise, 1:1 token	Goal 2nd R+ schedule: 1:2 praise, 1:2 token for independent responses

Generalization (**stimulus factors**): [people, place, materials, supervision, etc.] Vary staff, directions, activities (e.g., cooking, art, gym), and locations	Generalization (**response factors**): [rate, accuracy, magnitude, duration etc.] Increase distance to items

Parametric details: Work on this skill within other activities such as cooking, gym, circle, trips, and art. Give the student the direction (e.g., while cooking: "Put the bottle in the refrigerator.", "Get a bowl.", "Stir.", while in art: "Get the scissors.", Get the ____ paint.", etc.) and fully prompt him/her to complete the direction. Fade the intensity of prompting to partial physical and then to a gesture as the student becomes more independent with the task direction. Indicate the level of prompt given or "+" if completed independently. Be sure to mix up activities, directions, materials, items, and settings so you can be sure that the student is following the direction given and not just responding because they know what to do with a particular object, heard a key word, or has learned what to do in a particular setting or situation, etc.

Data Collection

Date	Staff	Activity	Direction given	Prompt level	Comments
3/1	Sandy	snack	Give me your cup	+	
3/1	Donna	snack	Put plate in trash	FP	
3/2	Jan	gym	Go line up	PP	
3/3	Jim	lunch	Wipe your mouth	+	Awesome!
3/4	Jan	arrival	Pick up your coat	+	
3/5	Donna	snack	Throw away trash	+	
3/5	Sandy	bathroom	Close the door	G	
3/5	Jim	going outside	Get your coat	+	
3/8	Sandy	going to music	Line up	PP	
3/10	Jim	groups	Go to Sandy	PP	Ran into hallway
3/10	Jan	Rec/leisure	Clean up the cars	+	
3/11	Jim	lunch	Go get your lunch	G	
3/13	Donna	transitions	Wait	PP, PP, G, +, G	Direction given 4x's today

Response Key

Correct: +
Incorrect: -
No response: NR

	100											
	90											
	80											
	70											
	60											
	50											
	40											
	30											
	20											
	10											
	date	3/1	3/2		3/4	3/5	3/8	3/9	310	3/11	3/13	

Prompt Level Key

FP = full physical
PP = partial physical
M = model
G = gesture
PV = partial verbal
FV = full verbal

142

Pyramid Educational Consultants

Discrete Lesson Plan		Target Skill:	Indicating 'finished'	

Student:		Teacher:		Date:

Behavior objective: When the student has completed an activity, he/she will let a staff member know by exchanging a "finished" picture or by saying "finished"/"I'm finished".
  Functional association: Domain: Communication   Function: communication skills, independent work skills

Current lesson status [acquisition, fluency, maintenance]: acquisition
(trials/set; # data-points collected per week): 1 trial/set, 3 data points per week
Target Criterion (specify type of data: %, frequency, rate, duration, etc.): <1 prompt/5 trials, 3 staff, 4 activities

Current **Stimulus Control**: Needs full physical prompting	Long-term **cue**: Work completed

Discrete Trial format: Yes [maximum # per set] 1 trial/set	Sequential format: No Chained?: No

One vs. Two person prompt?: **Two**	**Prompt Strategy**: Fading - FP, PP, M, G Pause interval (for hierarchy or delayed):

Error Correction:

Natural or additional completion R+: praise, access to next activity, edible	2nd R+ (during task): n/a
Current 2nd R+ schedule: 1:1 praise, 1:1 small edible	Goal 2nd R+ schedule: 1:3 praise

Generalization (**stimulus factors**): [people, place, materials, supervision, etc.] Vary staff, activities being completed (e.g., folding laundry, legos, sorting utensils), work locations, fade trainer	Generalization (**response factors**): [rate, accuracy, magnitude, duration, etc.]

Parametric details: Work on this skill with activities that have a clearly defined endpoint (e.g., using up all the legos in a bowl, folding all the towels in a basket). Initially, when the student completes an activity the communicative partner approaches him/her while the trainer prompts the student to indicate "finished". The communicative partner provides the reinforcement. Fade the trainer prompts and then the trainer as appropriate. Fade the proximity of the communicative partner so that the student learns to approach him/her to indicate that he/she is finished with the activity/work.

Data Collection

Date	Trainer	CO	Proximity of CP	Prompt level	activity	%	Comments
1/1	Emma	Erin	1 foot	FP FP FP PP PP	sorting	0	
1/2	Erin	Sue	1 foot	FP + + + +	groups	20	
1/3	Sue	Dave	1 foot	+ + G + +	puzzles	20	
1/7	Dave	Erin	1 foot	+ PP + + +	play cars	20	
1/8	Erin	Josh	1 1/2 feet	+ G G + +	snack	20	
1/9	Erin	Sue	2 feet	G +	snack	30	
1/15	Dave	Josh	2 feet	+ +	groups	20	
1/17	Emma	Erin	2. 5 feet	PP PP + + PP	puzzle	20	
1/23	Josh	Emma	2.5 feet	PP + + + +	snack	20	
1/24	Sue	Josh	2.5 feet	+ + +	groups	20	

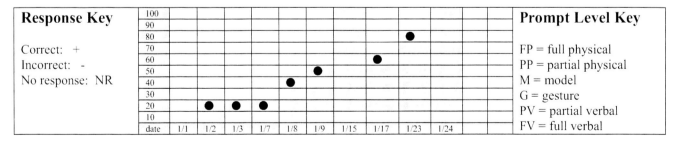

Response Key

Correct: +
Incorrect: -
No response: NR

| | 1/1 | 1/2 | 1/3 | 1/7 | 1/8 | 1/9 | 1/15 | 1/17 | 1/23 | 1/24 | | |

Prompt Level Key

FP = full physical
PP = partial physical
M = model
G = gesture
PV = partial verbal
FV = full verbal

We collect data for the purpose of monitoring an individual's progress or lack thereof. By frequently evaluating our data, we can catch a student who is not making progress and make the necessary changes to the lesson. If we do not evaluate our data, the outcome could be to the detriment of student who is stagnating without learning. Also, by evaluating the data, a teacher can monitor whether the lesson is a good one and help identify those positive elements that can be incorporated into other lessons. Similarly, if it is not a good lesson, then we can begin to determine what was not effective.

It is not always necessary to take trial-by-trial data. It is only necessary to take enough data that it adequately represents the current status of the student's progress. This status can be illustrated is by a trend line once the data are put into graphic form. There are several different types of trend lines: increasing trend line, decreasing trend line, and a zero trend line. It is only necessary to take enough data to establish a reliable trend line. Typically, more data is taken during the early trials of a lesson to closely monitor how the student is doing with the skill. We typically do not take as much data when the student is demonstrating skill-acquisition, the skill is in maintenance, and/or within some types of generalization. Discussed below are the three different types of trend lines, what these trend lines tell us about a student's progress, as well as what possible changes could be made to turn a decreasing trend into an increasing trend.

The first lesson plan - *make cookies* - represents data indicative of a student making progress, as illustrated by the graph and the **increasing trend line**. As outlined by the lesson plan, the prompting strategy is a most-to-least hierarchy; therefore, the teacher initially provides the greatest amount of assistance and then reduces assistance as the student's progress (independence) increases. A backward chain is indicated, so the last step of the task analysis will be taught first while the other steps are prompted through. The data and the trend illustrate a student gradually making progress in independently completing the individual steps of the task analysis (from the back of the chain forward). According to the criteria designated on the lesson plan, the target is 80% accuracy, across two different staff members, and with a total of two different types of cookies. Our data indicates that criteria were obtained on 3/9 and again on 3/14 with two different staff members. Confirmation is still needed as to whether there were two different types of cookies because that was not documented on the data sheet. Because the student continues to make progress, no changes to the implementation practices of this plan need to be made at this time. However, because the student is doing so well, generalization factors (both stimulus and response) need to be considered and implemented (if not already in place). For example, making the cookies in different locations, making twice as many cookies, and using different cookie sheets.

The second lesson plan - *follow one step spoken directions* - represents a student who was initially making progress but due to variables yet to be defined, is not continuing to do so. The decreasing trend line on the graph illustrates this change. If you were to just scan the raw data on the data sheet (i.e., *eyeing it up),* you might conclude that the student is doing all right because there are some independent responses documented. However, it is not until the graph is completed that the real picture is illustrated. The progress the student had made is quickly decreasing. The graph indicates that changes need to be made to the plan so the student can better acquire the skill. One of the considerations that need to be examined is the prompting strategy. Is there another strategy that would be more effective? Is the current one being implemented correctly? Another element of the lesson that needs to be looked at is the error correction. Is it being implemented? Is it being implemented correctly and consistently? Is another error correction more suitable? Still another consideration is the reinforcement. Is the reinforcer powerful enough to motivate the student? Is there a more effective one? Is the 'deal' (LMAD) being set prior to the demand? Is the reinforcer being delivered in a timely manner (e.g., 1/2 second rule)? Is enough reinforcement being delivered? Additionally, the data collected can be analyzed at other levels. For example, the data indicate that there are a variety of staff implementing the lesson, within a variety of activities, and that 13 different directions are currently being taught. Based on this total evaluation, it is important to first make sure that there are no training issues involved regarding the prompting strategy, error correction, or the delivery of reinforcement. If procedures listed in the plan were reliably implemented then changes in the plan would be warranted. In addition, perhaps limiting the number of activities targeted early in the lesson and concentrating only on a maximum of 2-4 different directions at one time would be beneficial. Additional directions can be introduced as the student gains correct responses to the current array. These changes would be made first before decisions to change other aspects of the plan were made. A time of 2-3 weeks to re-evaluate the data would be sufficient to assess the effectiveness of the changes.

The third lesson plan - *indicating finished* - illustrates a **zero trend line** and a student that is not really making progress, but is averaging around 50% independent. According to the data, the student is requiring a variety of prompts, some more intrusive than others. Again, if you were just *eyeing it up,* you might conclude that there are some independent responses and therefore the student is making progress; however, once again, the graph illustrates a different picture. Indeed, the student has made some progress, but the trend line seems to indicate that the student will continue to hover around 50% unless teaching practices are more closely evaluated and subsequently changed. As stated previously, some of the considerations of the plan that need to be evaluated include: prompting strategy, error correction, reinforcement, reinforcement schedules, and staff training issues. In addition to examining these elements, it is also beneficial to evaluate the current data. The data indicate that the objective is being implemented across a variety of staff (all of whom are participating as both the trainer and the communicative partner), across a variety of activities, and that the proximity of the communicative partner varies so that the student has to travel in order to communicate "finished." In order to effect a change on the trend line, and subsequently increase the success of the student, the following alterations could first be made: target only a few activities/work situations, minimize the distance the student has to travel in order to communicate they are finished (e.g., 1-2 feet, across a table), and follow the recommendation in the parametric details section of the plan making sure the activities being targeted have clearly defined endings. After making these modifications, implementation should continue for another couple of weeks until the student's progress can be re-evaluated.